THE GRANTWRITER'S
INTERNET
COMPANION

CORWIN
PRESS

The Corwin Press logo—a raven striding across an open book—represents the happy union of courage and learning. We are a professional-level publisher of books and journals for K–12 educators, and we are committed to creating and providing resources that embody these qualities. Corwin's motto is "Success for All Learners."

THE GRANTWRITER'S INTERNET COMPANION

A
Resource
for
Educators
and Others
Seeking
Grants
and
Funding

Susan Peterson

CORWIN PRESS, INC.
A Sage Publications Company
Thousand Oaks, California

For information:

Corwin Press, Inc.
A Sage Publications Company
2455 Teller Road
Thousand Oaks, California 91320
CORWIN   E-mail: order@corwinpress.com
PRESS

Sage Publications Ltd.
6 Bonhill Street
London EC2A 4PU
United Kingdom

Sage Publications India Pvt. Ltd.
M-32 Market
Greater Kailash I
New Delhi 110 048 India

Printed in the United States of America

Library of Congress Cataloging-in-Publication Data

Peterson, Susan Louise, 1960-
    The grantwriter's internet companion: A resource for educators and others seeking grants and funding / by Susan Peterson.
        p. cm.
    Includes index.
    ISBN 0-7619-7808-9 (cloth)
    ISBN 0-7619-7746-5 (paper)
    1. Educational fund raising—United States. 2. Proposal writing for grants—United States. 3. Proposal writing in education—United States. 4. Interned in education—United States. I. Title.
    LC243.A1 P48 2001
    370'.0681—dc21   00-010949

This book is printed on acid-free paper.

01   02   03   04   05   10   9   8   7   6   5   4   3   2   1

Corwin Editorial Assistant: Julia Parnell
Production Editor: Denise Santoyo
Editorial Assistant: Cindy J. Bear
Typesetter/Designer: Barbara Burkholder
Indexer: Kathy Paparchontis

Contents

About the Author

Susan Peterson, PhD, is Director of the Center for Academic Excellence at the University of Central Arkansas (UCA) in Conway, Arkansas. She has written and received numerous grants and served on grantwriting teams for schools and non-profit agencies. She conducts inservice sessions for educators and others about grantwriting—specifically, about making use of the Internet to research funding sources, data, and grantwriting tips.

Susan Peterson also has served as a reader for national and state grants and as program evaluator for Even Start and other family literacy grants in Arkansas. Her curiosity in writing this manual stemmed from the curiosity shown by educators, especially teachers, who wanted to learn more about locating funding sources and writing grants.

Before joining the Center, Peterson taught reading, language arts, and curriculum courses in the elementary and secondary education departments at UCA. She continues to be an advocate for literacy and served as president of the Arkansas State Reading Association (ARA), an affiliate of the International Reading Association, in 1992 and is currently the ARA state coordinator. She has served on the boards of Nonprofit Resources, Inc. and the Faulkner County Literacy Council.

She received her BS and MEd from Clarion University in Pennsylvania and her PhD from the University of Akron, with additional course work in curriculum and supervision at the University of Pittsburgh. She taught English and reading in elementary and secondary schools in Pennsylvania for 8 years. Her publications have appeared in *The Executive Educator, The National Middle School Journal, The Reading Teacher, First Teacher, Clearing House, SubJournal, The Reader,* and other state and national journals.

Introduction

————▶ ◀————

J ust a few years ago, if I were asked to present an inservice session about writing grants, I would prepare multiple pages of information for handouts. When asked to do the same presentation now, I can provide those in attendance with much more information—simply by arming them with the power of the Internet.

Today, administrators and central office personnel are not the only educators writing grants. Classroom teachers are finding that grants can provide an excellent source of funding for special classroom projects, school-wide programs, and even personal growth opportunities. Typically, teachers who have written grants have found the experience very empowering, and they want to know how to find additional funding sources and grantwriting assistance.

This publication is not designed to be a how-to on grantwriting. Rather, the intent is to assist educators and others interested in grantwriting to use the Internet as a resource that will help locate funding sources and other sites that may prove useful when seeking funding.

It is only through practice that one builds confidence in using the Internet. Knowing and using effective search strategies can make the difference between finding good "hits" and getting the exact information you want or becoming frustrated

It should be noted that the Internet is in a constant state of transformation and that some of the sites listed in this publication may have changed addresses—or even disappeared completely! All due effort was made to include only those sites that the author believes will be sustained over time.

ACKNOWLEDGMENTS

The contributions of the following reviewers are gratefully acknowledged:

Mandy Brooks
Professor
Youngstown State University
Akron, OH

David Frankel
Technology Consultant
Wayne County RESA
Wayne, MI

Philip Bennett
Dean, School of Education
Lander University
Greewood, SC

Anita Davis
Professor & Chair of Education
Converse College
Spartanburg, SC

Bobby Capwell
Teacher
K. E. Little Elementary School
Bacliff, TX

Sandra Hildreth
Art Methods Instructor,
Education Department
St. Lawrence University
Canton, NY

Dr. Kevin Hopkins
Associate Professor,
Math Department Chair
Southwest Baptist University
Bolivar, MO

1

The Internet Advantage

According to Microsoft's *History of the Internet*, it all began about 30 years ago when the U.S. Department of Defense laid the foundation of the Internet with a network called ARPANET. However, it wasn't until the development of the World Wide Web in the early 1990s that the general public began to use the Internet and its various components.

Government, commercial, nonprofit, and educational organization Websites, or home pages, are expanding at a rapid pace. It's hard to believe that in June 1993, there were only 130 Websites. Now there are millions, and the number continues to burgeon (http://www.microsoft.com/insider/articles/history/htm).

According to NetSizer (http://www.netsizer.com), a Website that provides daily Internet statistics, the number of registrants in the Internet's Domain Name Service, or DNS, increased from approximately 43 million in January of 1999 to more than 66 million by the year 2000.

With the Web's easy navigation and accessibility in both school and home settings, anyone can find an unlimited amount of information. Educators are finding many uses for the Internet, especially as a resource to locate information, to develop curriculum, and to communicate with peers. And as individuals become more proficient in using the Internet, their expertise in locating specific information becomes more refined and focused.

Today, education professionals and others who are looking for funding are discovering that the Internet is a remarkable resource. Using the Internet, anyone can easily locate information that in the past was available only to those in professional grantseeker circles or to those with enough perseverance to study expensive publications that could be found only in certain libraries.

Now, anyone can easily access specific grant information or uncover the how-tos of grantwriting in general. Information abounds on federal and private grant sources, grantwriting tips, grant applications, and winning grant proposal samples. Data to support the need for a project can be found at the touch of a button. Whether one is a novice or an experienced grantwriter, the Internet can be a powerful tool that can assist in numerous ways. Its advantages include the following:

- Quick, easy access to a vast array of information
- Relatively low cost (especially as compared with print sources)
- Accessibility in rural or remote areas
- Savings of time and money (versus postage and long-distance phone costs)
- 24-hour availability

The World Wide Web (*WWW* or *the Web*) is the fastest growing activity on the Internet. However, other Internet services are also available, such as electronic mail (*e-mail*) and access to electronic discussion groups that are often called *listservs*, after the original software that managed e-mail lists. The information found in this manual focuses on the Web, but other services are mentioned as well.

This publication is not intended to be a grantwriting manual, nor a manual on how to use the Internet. It is presumed that the user has a basic understanding of the Internet and has a connection to it. The following tips may prove useful, however:

The address of any Website is its URL (Universal Resource Locator). The *http://* is the standard preface, or protocol, used in URLs, and depending on your computer, you may not need to type *http://www* on the address line. In other words, it may be possible to access the U.S. Department of Education's Web page by typing only *ed.gov* on the address line rather than *http://www.ed.gov.* Try it, and see which works for you.

By using addresses that are provided in this publication and typing them into the address box of your Web browser, you can access numerous sites that are directly or indirectly related to writing grants. The sites that seem most useful can be stored as either bookmarks or "favorites," depending on which Web browser you use. The two most well-known Web browsers are Netscape Navigator and Microsoft Internet Explorer. Learn how to add and delete your favorite sites and to organize them into folders on your computer.

Don't waste money buying expensive books on how to navigate the Internet. Simply click on your browser's Help button and skim your system's tutorial to assist you in learning these functions.

A helpful site for those interested in various facets of the Internet is found at the University of Oklahoma at http://www.ou.edu/research/electron/internet/. Here are user-friendly links to sites dealing with such issues as privacy and security, e-mail virus updates, use of e-mail and video, computer glossaries, tutorials, and general information.

Although the Internet allows you to communicate with computer users around the world in order to access information, it should be noted that some information remains hard to find and that, sometimes, the information you find can be wrong. Always be sure to assess the source of the information you intend to use and to evaluate data for timeliness and accuracy.

2

---◆---

Learning to Look

The World of Search Engines

Using the Internet to locate grant information is _____.

A. fun
B. fascinating
C. frustrating
D. all of the above

If you've ever looked for specific information on the Internet, you know the answer is D. Yes, searching for information on the Web can be exciting and fun . . . but it also can be very frustrating if you don't know effective search strategies. Newcomers to the Internet often experience a lot of frustration, especially when looking for specific information rather than simply surfing.

Most of us probably conducted our first search by clicking on the Search button that accompanies Internet Explorer or Netscape Navigator. A *search engine* is a tool for locating information about any topic. These engines "crawl" through Websites, looking for a key word or phrase that you provide, and then within seconds, they create a list of Websites for you to explore. (Technology experts would point out that there is a difference between the way that search engines and directories operate; however, for the purpose of this publication, both will be referred to as search engines, as is common practice.)

The two basic types of search engines are based on topics (or subject trees) or key words. Topic or subject tree search engines generate a list of topics, and the topics are narrowed in focus by clicking on a word or phrase. In key word search engines, a word or phrase is typed into the search line.

The following is a list of some major search engines. Their popularity is based on their ease of use and dependability. They are more likely to be well maintained and regularly upgraded because of their commercial backing.

- Yahoo: http://www.yahoo.com
- AltaVista: http://www.altavista.digital.com
- Infoseek: http://www.infoseek.com
- Lycos: http://www.lycos.com
- Excite: http://www.excite.com
- Hotbot: http://www.hotbot.com

There are, literally, hundreds of search engines. But just as different libraries have different collections, the same is true of search engines. Each search engine has its own type of holdings, its own strengths and weaknesses. Never assume that what you find (or don't find) with one search engine is all that is available on the Internet.

For a really thorough search, try using a meta- (or multiple) search engine. A relatively user-friendly metasearch engine, and personal favorite, is Dogpile (http://www.dogpile.com). This site searches approximately 22 search engines at one time, including those just mentioned. After typing your key word or phrase, click on the Fetch (rather than Search) button to have "Arfie" return your list of sites. The sites are displayed by search engine, and you have the choice of going deeper into each search engine's results or of viewing the top hits found by the next search engine.

Other well-known or long-established metasearch engines are the following:

- Go2Net/MetaCrawler: http://www.go2net.com
- SavvySearch: http://www.savvysearch.com
- Inference Find: http://www.infind.com
- Mamma: http://www.mamma.com

It is interesting to compare the different sites that each search engine finds because the returns are often very diverse. Some engines are great at locating a keyword, but they have no ability whatsoever to find synonyms. Others may locate synonyms but are more likely to find lots of pages you don't want. Yahoo is good at finding the most popular pages.

LOOKING FOR GRANT WHO?

It may seem logical to type the word *grant* into a key word search engine if you're looking for information about grants. However, anyone who has tried this strategy knows that it does not yield a very effective return. Interspersed with a few promising sites will be information about Amy Grant, Cary Grant, Grant County, and hundreds of other *grant*s not even considered. Unfortunately, the computer cannot yet intuit what we really intend to say when a word has multiple meanings. But the effective researcher knows how to communicate clearly, using computer language (or syntax), in order for the computer to provide the searcher with meaningful *hits*, or results in the form of Websites.

Typically, a search engine will have a button on its home page that leads to tips to make your search more successful. These links are generally labeled as *search tips, help with search-*

ing, or *help with syntax*. If you are truly serious about finding specific information, take the time to visit the search engine's search tips. . . you will save time later, and your search will yield better results.

Knowing a few simple search techniques that are supported by most search engines may help to increase your returns. If the tips provided later in the chapter need further explanation, or if you wish to become more informed about search engines in general, visit Search Engine Watch (http://www.searchenginewatch.com). You can become a search engine guru by studying features of major search engines, reading about power searches and Boolean searches, and comparing the pros and cons of various search commands and search engines.

When looking for information about funding sources, try using some creative words or phrases. Try adapting the following search tips to your own needs.

1. Use quotation marks to keep words or phrases together.
2. In Boolean search strategies, use the capitalized words *AND, OR, NOT*, and *NEAR* to connect words.
3. Use + or – before a word (to indicate inclusion or exclusion of the word).
4. Use * as a wildcard to stand in for word parts.

Here are some examples:

- "successful proposals"
- *grants AND mathematics* (Boolean search words remain capitalized)
- *grant +literacy* (note that there is no space after the + or – sign)
- *"fund* proposals"* (using the * could pull up funds, funded, and funding)

- *grants +humanities –music OR "humanities grants" -music* (will return information on humanities grants, excluding music)
- *"foundation grants" +technology*
- *"family literacy programs" "funding agenc*"* (Here, the * would allow the word agency or agencies.)
- *"New Orleans" +foundations* (Try using your city or state.)

Performing a search using the phrase *grant writing* will undoubtedly yield a large number of hits and a more qualified return than simply entering the word *grant*. Unfortunately, many of the returned sites will likely be (a) someone who is selling a grantwriting service, (b) individuals advertising products about grantwriting, or (c) businesses promoting various types of assistance to grantwriters. Sorting through these sites can be time consuming and discouraging, especially if the name and description of a site seem to be a perfect match.

One approach to countering this problem is to develop a skill in reading addresses, or URLs. By understanding domain categories, you can get an idea of the type of site that will be most helpful for your needs. Most domain categories that appear at the end of the address to a primary Web page include the following abbreviations:

- *.org—nonprofit organizations*
- *.edu—educational sites*
- *.gov—government sites*
- *.com—commercial (or business) sites*
- *.net—networks*
- *.mil—military services*
- *.int—organizations established by international treaty*

Thus, someone wanting to purchase products or services would most likely find the *.com* sites useful, whereas those searching for direct links to foundations would most likely be looking for nonprofit organizations, indicated by *.org*.

CONCLUSION

Without effective search strategies, many hours can be spent on the Internet looking for specific information. Search engines vary greatly according to the materials they contain, how they are organized, and how they are used. Take time to try various engines, experiment with different search terms and tools, and compare findings provided by various search engines. Eventually, the engines that respond best to your searches will become those that you will rely upon and return to most often.

TIME FOR RECESS

Ever wonder what others are searching for? Go to Magellan Search Voyeur (http://voyeur.mckinley.com/cgi-bin/voyeur.cgi) and take a peek at the information that others are looking for! (Consider this an opportunity to see search tips applied.) Every 15 seconds, this site displays samples of real-time searches. The *Lycos 50 Daily Report* at http://50.Lycos.com/ displays the 50 most popular Lycos user searches for the week.

3

Finding the Big Bucks

U. S. Department of Education

The U.S. Department of Education (ED; http://www.ed.gov) is the agency of the U.S. government that administers federal funds for education programs, conducts and disseminates education research, and focuses national attention on issues and problems in education.

According to the "Budget" home page of the U.S. Department of Education, the Department currently administers a budget of about $38 billion per year. (That amount, by the way, is approximately 2% of the $1.8 trillion federal budget.) The Department pursues its twin goals of access and excellence through the administration of 175 programs that touch on every area and level of education. Department programs provide grant, loan, and work-study assistance to more than 8 million postsecondary students.

Finding grants and funding information on the Department's home page (see Figure 3.1) is relatively easy and can be approached in several ways. On the left side of the home page, there is a Funding Opportunities link that goes directly to informational sites and offices. (You can bypass the home page and go directly to the Funding Opportunities page by using this URL: http://www. ed.gov/funding.html.) Beneath the Most Requested Items. . . heading, there is a Discretionary Grant Applications link that lists application packages available for grant competitions that are currently open and for which the grants are available on the basis of a competitive process (unlike formula grants).

Congress establishes discretionary grant programs through a legislative and appropriations process. Six offices in the Department are responsible for program administration and oversight. These are as follows:

- Office of Bilingual Education and Minority Languages Affairs (OBEMLA)
- Office of Educational Research and Improvement (OERI)
- Office of Elementary and Secondary Education (OESE)
- Office of Postsecondary Education (OPE)
- Office of Special Education and Rehabilitative Services (OSERS)
- Office of Vocational and Adult Education (OVAE)

Let's first explore the Discretionary Grants Applications (found under ED's "Most Requested Items" heading). Here you will find funding opportunites that are available *right now!* At the time of this writing, 29 discretionary grants are listed, all of which support the Department's priorities and initiatives. These include:

Figure 3.1. ED's Home Page

ED's home page is described as both an online library and newsstand.

There are four main sections to the home page:

1. Across the top, there are *tools to assist searching*.
2. Along the left side, there are major *categories*, such as the President's Priorities, Funding, Financial Aid for College, Research and Statistics, Programs, Offices, Budget, and so on.
3. In the center are *headlines*.
4. At the bottom is a list of *most requested items*.

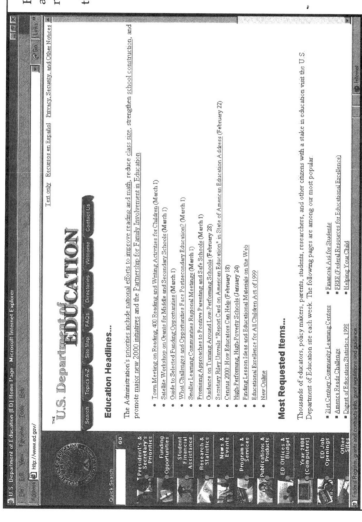

Note: Titles of available Discretionary Grant packages (below) will change throughout the year.

- Learning Anytime Anywhere Partnerships
- Research Institute to Enhance the Role of Special Education and Children With Disabilities in Education Policy Reform
- Vocational Rehabilitation Service Projects for American Indians With Disabilities
- Directed Research Projects
- 21st Century Community Learning Centers Program
- Fund for the Improvement of Postsecondary Education
- Partnerships in Character Education Pilot Projects
- Bilingual Education: State Grant Program
- Visiting Scholars Fellowship Program

If the title of the program is of interest to you, simply click on the title to receive its summary. Before reading about a program in detail, look for three pieces of information: closing date, applicant eligibility, and expected number of grants to be awarded. If this information is not in the summary, go to the Forecast of Funding Opportunities link, which is found under the Funding Opportunities heading on ED's homepage. Always check to be sure that you (or the institution you represent) are an eligible applicant before spending time reading about a program—some grants are open only to state education agencies (SEAs), to higher education agencies (HEAs), or to local education agencies or school districts (LEAs). The number of grants awarded can be an indicator of its competitiveness. If it is not possible to meet the deadline for the current year, try to find out if the competition will be open the following year.

If interested in a grant, link to the Federal Register notice to find more information about the programs's priorities. Study these carefully to find if your needs match the priorities of the grant.

Box 3.1

Some federal programs give priority to Empowerment Zones and Enterprise Communities, abbreviated as EZ/EC. To see a map of EZ/EC communities, and to find out more about this program, visit http://www.ezec.gov. This site was developed by the EZ/EC Program Offices of the U.S. Department of Agriculture and the U.S. Department of Housing and Urban Development.

If you have any questions about a program or about your or your institution's eligibility, simply phone or e-mail the program's contact person—after all, it's his or her job to award all available funds. Most are very helpful, direct, and timely in responding to inquiries.

If the closing date of a program indicates that it may be doable and if all else is a good match for your idea, then download and print the application along with any other documents and forms that are needed to begin the federal application process. Most files can be downloaded in Microsoft Word or in the portable data format (PDF); the latter is most commonly read with Adobe Acrobat. Keep in mind that some federal programs are cyclical and will be repeated in future years. Missing a deadline one year may simply mean that you have additional time to prepare for it the next. Again, do your homework to see whether the grant will be awarded in future years, or call the program's contact person.

Box 3.2

The Department does suggest that applicants request an official copy of the package because important information may be scrambled when downloading the electronic version. Also, if there is a change in the competition, they will know where to contact you.

Although it's fun and interesting to view what programs (and monies) are currently available, it's also a good idea to do some homework and find out more about federal programs and how they operate. To do this, click on the Funding Opportunities button on the Department's home page. From this point, you can click on the following links.

Discretionary Grant Application Packages. As previously mentioned, these pages list grant competitions that are currently open and provide links to downloadable application packages, forms, and other information that you will need to apply.

Federal Register Documents. These include notices inviting applications for grant competitions, as well as funding priorities, selection criteria, regulations, and relevant workshops and meetings. More information on the *Federal Register* can be found in Chapter 4.

FY 2000 Forecast of Funding Opportunities Under ED Discretionary Grant Programs. Lists the dates, estimated number of awards, and funding amounts for virtually all the Department's direct-grant and fellowship competitions for new awards. This site gives a good overview of the programs in an easy-to-view table format.

What Should I Know About ED Grants. A useful starting place, especially for the novice grantwriter, is the user-friendly ED publication, *What Should I Know About ED Grants*, which is also directly accessible at http://www.ed. gov/pubs/KnowAbtGrants/. According to its title page, this booklet provides a nontechnical summary of the Department of Education's discretionary grants process and the laws and regulations that govern it. In essence, it is the department's attempt to demystify the grants process. The easy-to-read, question-and-answer format supplies answers to those most-often-asked questions that cover such topics as how to apply for and make use of federal grant funds, reporting pro-cedures, site visits, and what to do if you're audited. But what may be most helpful to newcomers interested in federal grants is the glossary of grant-related words that explains the many phrases, acronyms, and abbreviations that have become part of the alphabet soup of federal funding. Scroll down to the bottom of the page to find the glossary, or go to http://ed.gov/pubs/KnowAbtGrants/glossary. html.

Guide to ED Programs. Provides a concise description of each of the programs administered by the Department of Edu-cation, identifies who may apply, and gives the name and tele-phone number of the ED office to contact for more informa-tion. About 175 programs are listed here, and you can search for programs according to applicant type (individual, non-profit organization, higher education agency, etc.).

ED General Administrative Regulations (EDGAR). Defines the administrative requirements for managing projects funded by discretionary grants awarded by ED.

Grants and Contracts Information. Provides additional information including currently available contract solicita-tions, a forecast of upcoming contract opportunities, grants policy bulletins, and databases of contract and grant awards.

Take advantage of the award databases for grants and contracts to find out the *who, what, when,* and *where* about grants that have been awarded nationally or in your area! The award dates, amounts, and contact persons are all available to you (sorted by state, contract number, congressional dis-trict, etc.). This information can be accessed directly at http://ocfo.ed.gov/grntinfo/grntawd.htm or by linking through the ED home page (http://www.ed.gov): → Funding Opportu-nities → Grants and Contract Information → Grants Informa-tion → Grant Awards Database. It is very useful to view descriptions of awards and contracts that have been previously funded, and doing this kind of homework in advance will help you determine whether there is a general match between your proposed activity and the types of awards or types of organizations that are generally funded.

Box 3.3

When Shari Coston from Pulaski County Special School District in Little Rock heard about the 21st Century Community Learning Centers (21st CCLC) initiative for after-school programs, it sounded almost too good to be true. But she searched the Grants and Contracts database and found that six Arkansas schools had received funds that averaged $200,000 per school during the first and second years of the program. (Nationally, approximately $60 and $133 million dollars were awarded, respectively.) Using grants and contracts information found on the Internet, she found who in the state received funding. She then contacted them to discuss details on applying for and managing programs. By studying copies of previously funded grants, which she downloaded from the Internet, she examined how goals and objectives were written and how evaluations would be conducted. When visiting 21st CCLC's home page (http://ed.gov/21stcclc/), she was alerted to a workshop, or Bidder's Conference, to assist new applicants. She also found a link on the home page to the National Center for Community Education (http://www.nccenet.org) where she found additional ideas to help develop her proposal.

All her Internet detective work paid off—the program, was awarded first year funding in the amount of $319,914.

PROGRAM OFFICES OF THE
U.S. DEPARTMENT OF EDUCATION

To understand more about the organization of the Department of Education and to link to the various program offices, visit http://www.ed.gov/gen_ed_org/ or http://www.ed.gov/offices/. The program offices include the following two, in addition to the six already mentioned at the beginning of the chapter:

- Office for Civil Rights (OCR)
- Office of Student Financial Assistance Programs (OSFAP)

Many of the departments have responsibility for administering funding opportunities that include formula and discretionary grants and contracts. Each department can be directly accessed by using *http://www.ed.gov/offices/*, followed by the department's initials between two backslash characters. For example, the OESE can be directly accessed at http://www.ed.gov/offices/OESE/.

The Office of Elementary and Secondary Education. Includes offices that provide financial assistance to state and local educational agencies for maintenance and improvement of both public and private preschool, elementary, and secondary education. Their programs include Class Size Reduction, Compensatory Education, Comprehensive School Reform Demonstration, Goals 2000, Impact Aid, Indian Education, Migrant Education, Reading Excellence, Safe and Drug-Free Schools, and School Improvement.

The Office of Bilingual Education and Minority Languages Affairs. Offers state grants and other programs, including Teachers and Personnel, Career Ladder, Training for All Teachers, Systemwide Improvement, Comprehensive School,

Program Enhancement, Program Development and Implementation, Foreign Language Assistance/LEA, Foreign Language Assistance/SEA, Immigrant Education, and Field Initiated Research.

The Office of Educational Research and Improvement. Strives to promote excellence and equity in American education by conducting research and demonstration projects funded through grants to help improve education. This office also collects statistics, distributes information, and provides technical assistance. The office administers five Institute programs to ensure that it carries out a coordinated and comprehensive program of research and development. Each Institute administers Field-Initiated Studies and other grant awards. The five Institutes are as follows:

1. The National Institute on Student Achievement, Curriculum, and Assessment (SAI) funds projects that address issues such as reducing and preventing school violence, technology in the schools, and improving teaching and learning. Their Website is http:// www.ed.gov/offices/OERI/SAI/.

2. The National Institute on the Education of At-Risk Students (At-Risk Institute) awards grants to institutions of higher education, regional educational laboratories, research institutions, and individual researchers. Projects focus on increasing achievement of students at risk of educational failure because of limited English proficiency, poverty, race, geographic location, or economic disadvantage. Their Website is http://www.ed.gov/offices/OERI/At-Risk/.

3. The National Institute on Early Childhood Development and Education (ECI) provides funding to hospitals, health centers, universities, and research organizations. Youth violence, children with disabilities, parenting and readiness,

cognitive development, language and literacy, and the use of technology in education are some of the areas of study funded by their grant programs. Their Website is http://www.ed.gov/offices/OERI/ECI/.

4. The National Institute on Educational Governance, Finance, Policymaking, and Management (Governance and Finance Institute) awards grants to universities and research organizations to study such topics as local reaction to state education reforms, charter schools and professional development schools, school choice policies, promoting harmony in schools, and professional development. Their Website is http://www.ed.gov/offices/OERI/GFI/.

5. The National Institute on Postsecondary Education, Libraries, and Lifelong Learning (PLLI) has awarded grants that deal with benefits of distance education, effective public library services in low-income areas, effective adult learning experiences, and effective faculty contributions to undergraduate learning. Their Website is http://www.ed.gov/offices/OERI/PLLI/.

The Office of Vocational and Adult Education. Provides useful information about programs, grants, and events on the following subjects: adult education, vocational education, national programs for vocational and adult education, School-to-Work, Community College Liaison Office, White House Initiative on Tribal Colleges and Universities, Office of Correctional Education, and Empowerment Zones/Enterprise Communities.

The Office of Special Education and Rehabilitative Services. Supports programs that assist in educating children with special needs, provides for the rehabilitation of youth and adults with disabilities, and supports research to improve the lives of individuals with disabilities through three pro-gram-related components: the Office of Special Education Programs (OSEP), the Rehabilitation Services Administration (RSA), and the National Institute on Disability and Rehabilita-tion Research (NIDRR).

1. The Office of Special Education Programs (OSEP) administers programs and projects relating to the free, appro-priate public education of all children, youth, and adults with disabilities, from birth through the age of 21. The bulk of spe-cial education funds is administered by OSEP's Monitoring and State Improvement Programs division, which provides grants to states and territories to assist them in providing a free, appropriate public education to all children with disabili-ties. The early intervention and preschool grant programs also provide grants to each state for children with disabilities, ages birth through five.

2. The Rehabilitation Services Administration (RSA) oversees programs to help disabled individuals obtain em-ployment through the provision of such supports as counsel-ing, medical and psychological services, job training, and other individualized services. The RSA's major formula grant program provides funds to state vocational rehabilitation agencies to provide employment-related services for individ-uals with disabilities, giving priority to individuals who are severely disabled.

3. The National Institute on Disability and Rehabilitation Research (NIDRR) provides a comprehensive program of research related to the rehabilitation of individuals with dis-abilities.

Another way to view available grants and contracts is to go directly to http://ocfo.ed.gov. (The department's Web server is managed by the Office of the Chief Financial Officer, hence the *ocfo* in the address.) At this location are current contract and grant opportunities, contract requests for proposals, forecasts for possible upcoming opportunities, instructions for being included on the contract bidders' mailing list, and other useful documents.

U.S. DEPARTMENT OF EDUCATION INITIATIVES

U.S. Department of Education fiscal year 2000 initiatives include the following:

Continuing Initiatives

Class Size Reduction—$1.3 billion in FY 2000. Helps school districts hire 100,000 teachers to reduce class sizes in Grades 1–3. Detailed information is available from WestEd at http://www.WestEd.org/policy/. For more information, e-mail class_size@ed.gov, or visit the Website, http://www.ed.gov offices/OESE/ClassSize/.

21st Century Community Learning Centers—$453.7 million in FY 2000. Funds school-community partnerships to keep community schools open after school and summers. For more information, e-mail 21stCCLC@ed.gov, or visit the Website at http://www.ed.gov/21stcclc/.

Reading Excellence—$260 million in FY 2000. Helps children learn to read well and independently by the end of the third grade. For more information, e-mail Reading_Excellence@ed.gov. Also, visit the Department's Website at http://www.ed.gov/offices/OESE/REA/.

Technology Literacy Challenge Fund—$425 million in FY 2000. Provides funds to states. For more information, visit the Website at http://www.ed.gov/Technology/TLCF/.

Safe and Drug Free Schools—Middle School Coordinators Program—$50 million in FY 2000. Enables middle schools to hire alcohol, drug, and violence prevention coordinators. For more information regarding this and other Safe and Drug Free Schools programs, visit the SDFS Website at http://www.ed.gov/offices/ OESE/SDFS/grants.html.

Comprehensive School Reform Demonstration Program—$220 million in FY 2000. Emphasis on basics and parental involvement to raise student achievement. For more information, e-mail compreform@ed.gov or visit the Website at http://www.ed. gov/offices/OESE/compreform.

Public Charter Schools Program—$145 million in FY 2000. Provides funds to states, which then award subgrants to charter school developers. For more information, visit the Website at http://www.uscharterschools.org.

Advanced Placement Incentive Program—$15 million in FY 2000. Enables states to reimburse part or all of the cost of test fees for eligible low-income individuals. For more information, visit the Website at http://aspe.os.dhhs. Gov/cfda/p84330.htm.

College Assistance Migrant Program (CAMP) and High School Equivalency Program (HEP)—$22 million combined in FY 2000. CAMP assists migrant and seasonal farm workers to complete the first academic year of college and succeed in postsecondary education. The High School Equivalency Program is designed to assist migrant and seasonal farm workers and their children to obtain a secondary school diploma or a General Equivalency Diploma certificate and to continue their postsecondary education or to enter career positions. For more information, visit the Office of Migrant Education (OME) Website at http://www.ed.gov/offices/OESE/MEP.

Teacher Quality Enhancement Grants—$98 million for FY 2000. Funds state projects that support systemic change in teacher licensure policies and practices and projects to recruit and prepare teachers. For more information, e-mail teacherquality@ed.gov, or visit the Website at http://www. ed. gov/offices/OPE/heatqp/.

Preparing Tomorrow's Teachers to Use Technology Program (PT3)—$75 million in FY 2000. A national teacher preparation reform initiative to ensure that all future teachers are technology-proficient educators who are well prepared to teach 21st-century students. For a complete list of the 225 grants or for more information on this program and the fiscal year 2000 grant competition, visit the PT3 Website at http://www.ed.gov/teachtech/, call (202) 502-7788, or send an e-mail to teacher_technology@ed.gov.

Bilingual Professional Development Program—$75 million in FY 2000. Its goal is to ensure that well-prepared personnel (teachers and others) are available to provide services to limited English-proficient students. For more information, visit the Website at http://www.ed.gov/offices/OBEMLA/fy2000.html.

GEAR UP for College Program—$200 million in FY 2000. A long-range early college preparation and awareness program that gives low-income students and their families pathways to college by partnering middle and high schools with colleges and community organizations. E-mail Gearup@ed.gov, or visit the Website at http://www.ed.gov/gearup.

Learning Anytime Anywhere Partnerships—$15 million in FY 2000. Supports postsecondary partnerships among colleges, businesses, and other organizations to promote technology-mediated distance education. For more information, e-mail LAAP@ed.gov, or visit the Website at http://www.ed. gov/offices/OPE/FIPSE/LAAP.

New American High Schools—$4 million in FY 2000. Showcases and supports outstanding high schools that have committed to extensive reform efforts, raised academic standards for all students, and achieved excellent results. For more information, visit the Website at http://www.ed.gov/ offices/OVAE/nahs/.

New Initiatives

Small Learning Communities Initiative—$45 million in FY 2000. These funds will be used for competitive grants to LEAs to plan, develop, and implement smaller learning communities for students in large high schools. For more information, contact Todd May at (202) 260-0960 or John Fiegel at (202) 260-2671. You can also visit the Website at http:// www.ed.gov/offices/OESE/SLCP/.

Elementary School Counseling Demonstration Program—$20 million in FY 2000. Funds will provide for establishment or expansion of counseling programs in elementary schools. For more information, visit http://www.ed.gov/offices/OESE/ SDFS/grants.html.

Safe and Drug Free Schools—Alternative Education Programs for Suspended and Expelled Youth—$10 million in FY 2000. Will help school districts identify effective procedures, policies, and programs that serve to discipline students without suspending or expelling them. Further information on the SDFS programs can be found at www.ed.gov/offices/OESE/ SDFS/grants.html.

American Indian Teacher Corps Professional Development Grants—$10 million in FY 2000. The American Indian Teacher Corps initiative combines several program elements in a manner that will effectively train 1,000 new teachers to work in schools with high concentrations of American Indian students. More information on the Office of Indian Education is available on their Website at http://www.eds.gov/offices/OESE/indian. html; however, there is no Internet information available about the grant itself.

CONCLUSION

Information about ED grants and services can be accessed directly through each program's Website or indirectly via the home page at http://www.ed.gov. First, become familiar with the organization of the Department of Education and its programs and priorities. Read the "What Should I Know About ED Grants" section and become familiar with the federal acronyms and grantwriting jargon. Investigate programs that might be most useful to your needs, then review what projects have been previously funded. Surfing the ED site can be time-consuming because of the amount of information; however, gaining an understanding of the department's priorities and knowing what has previously been funded may prevent you from wasting time on submitting a grant that is not likely to be funded.

Other ways to access information about ED grants are through the *Federal Register* and other publications (see Chapter 4) or by e-mailing lists to which you can subscribe (see Chapter 10).

4

Other Federal Agencies, Programs, and Publications

THE FEDERAL REGISTER

http://www.access.gpo.gov/su_docs/
aces/aces140.html
(Via the Government Printing Office)

http://www.nara.gov/fedreg/
(Via National Archives
and Records Administration)

The *Federal Register* is a legal newspaper published every business day by the National Archives and Records Administration (NARA). It contains federal agency regulations; proposed rules and notices; and Executive Orders, proclamations, and other presidential documents. The *Federal Register* informs citizens of their rights and obligations and provides access to a wide range of federal benefits and opportunities for funding.

NARA's Office of the Federal Register prepares the *Federal Register* for publication in partnership with the Government Printing Office (GPO), which distributes it in paper, on microfiche, and on the World Wide Web.

Because it can take 7 to 10 days to get a printed copy of the *Register* on library shelves, and because it is also quite expensive, with a yearly subscription price more than $500, the easiest way to access the Register and other government information is through the GPO's Internet access site, GPO Access, at http://www.access. gpo.gov.

The Government Printing Office (GPO), a part of the legislative branch of the federal government, produces numerous other publications in addition to the *Federal Register*. GPO Access is one of the few government Websites established by law and, established in 1994, is one of the longest running. According to their site, it is virtually the only government Website that provides easy, one-stop, no-fee access to information from all three branches of the government.

GPO Access links the public to over 105,000 titles on GPO's servers and to an additional 68,000 titles on other federal Websites. Their statistics indicate that more than 520 million documents have been retrieved by the public from GPO Access since its inception. Monthly document retrievals average more than 21 million, or about 924 gigabytes of information. Here you can find information ranging from nuclear regulation to reports from the intelligence community. Economic indicators, business and contracting opportunities, products, services, and, as previously mentioned, *The Federal Register,* are available here.

Each issue of the *Federal Register* is organized into four categories:

1. Presidential documents, including Executive Orders and proclamations
2. Rules and regulations, including policy statements and interpretations of rules

3. Proposed rules, including petitions for rule making and other advance proposals

4. Notices, including scheduled hearings and meetings open to the public, grant applications, and administrative orders

For a link to helpful hints on searching the *Federal Register,* visit http://www.access.gpo.gov/su_docs/aces/desc004. html. The NARA also offers an online tutorial for those interested in locating information in the daily *Federal Register* or the *Code of Federal Regulations.* To access the *Register* directly, visit the National Archives and Records Administration's Website at http://www.nara.gov/fedreg/.

The U.S. Department of Education's home page (http://www.ed.gov) also has an access link to the *Federal Register* under the Funding Opportunities heading. However, accessing the *Federal Register* through the ED site yields only documents published by the U.S. Department of Education. (This ED site can also be accessed at http://www.ed.gov/legislation/FedRegister/.) At the bottom of the page is a key word search (i.e., find *"all [ED] Federal Register documents which contain"* your key word). Keep in mind that this site will yield only Department of Education documents. If you want to expand your search to other agencies and programs beyond the Department of Education, go directly to the *Federal Register* or to the *Catalog of Federal Domestic Assistance* (discussed later in the chapter) at http:// www.cfda.gov or http://aspe.os. dhhs.gov/cfda/.

Known as the federal government's bible of funding opportunities, *The Catalog of Federal Domestic Assistance (CFDA)* can be accessed through various sites. This is a government-wide compendium of all federal programs, projects, services, and activities that provide assistance and benefits to U.S. citizens, including loans, loan guarantees, services, information, scholarships, training, and insurance.

The CFDA can be accessed at http://www.cfda.gov. By clicking on *search the catalog* and entering the keyword *grant*, an impressive listing of grants will appear. But by further limiting the search (for example, by using phrases such as *education grants* within quotation marks), more meaningful results will be achieved.

A second strategy is to access the site through the Department of Health and Human Services' (DHHS) key word index; the direct link to do this is as follows: http://aspe.os.dhhs.gov/cfda/. (*ASPE* is the Assistant Secretary for Planning and Evaluation, the principal advisor to the Secretary of the DHHS.) If you haven't used the Catalog before, read the "Introduction" to find information and tips on navigating the site. One advantage to the DHHS site is that programs are indexed topically. Simply scroll down to the Indexes heading to find grants organized by the following headings: Alphabetic Listing of Programs, Numeric Listing of Programs, Subject or Topic, Target or Beneficiary Group, Agency Within Department, and Independent and Other Agencies.

The Target or Beneficiary Group index is especially helpful, focusing on the type of individual your program will serve. There is a large choice of descriptors, broken down by age and other categories (*women, migrant, alcoholic*, for example).

The Subject or Topic category via the DHHS site lists 20 headings to choose from:

Agriculture

Food and Nutrition

Business and Commerce

Health

Community Development

Housing

Consumer Protection

Income Security and Social Services

Cultural Affairs

Information and Statistics

Disaster Prevention and Relief

Law, Justice, and Legal Services

Education

Natural Resources

Employment, Labor, and Training

Regional Development

Energy

Science and Technology

Environmental Quality

Transportation

Choosing the Education category leads to the following subcategories:

Dental Education and Training

Educational Equipment and Resources

Educational Facilities

Elementary and Secondary Education

General Research and Evaluation

Handicapped Education

Health Education and Training

Higher Education: General

Indian Education

Libraries and Technical Information Services

Medical Education and Training

Nuclear Education and Training

Nursing Education

Resource Development and Support: Elementary, Secondary Education

Resource Development and Support: General and Special Interest Organizations

Resource Development and Support: Higher Education

Resource Development and Support: Land and Equipment

Resource Development and Support: School Aid

Resource Development and Support: Sciences

Resource Development and Support: Student Financial Aid

Resource Development and Support: Vocational Education and Handicapped Education

Teacher Training

Vocational Development

As previously mentioned, most departments are interested in promoting educational programs, so do not restrict a search to the Education Department or to education categories only. For example, the Cultural Affairs category mentioned contains information under the subcategories Promotion of the Arts and Promotion of the Humanities, both of which have information that would interest humanities educators.

FEDERAL DEPOSITORY LIBRARIES

http://www.access.gpo.gov/su_docs/ locators/findlibs/ index.html

There are approximately 1,350 federal depository libraries throughout the United States and its territories, at least one in almost every congressional district. All provide free public access to a wide variety of federal government information in both print and electronic formats and have expert staff available to assist users. The library nearest you can be found by using the Website provided earlier.

COMMERCE BUSINESS DAILY

http://cbdnet.access.gpo.gov/index.html

CBDNet is the government's official, free, electronic version of the *Commerce Business Daily* (*CBD*), published by the U.S. Department of Commerce. The CBD does not deal with grant competitions directly, although some institutions and agencies may benefit from materials included in the CBD.

SOCIETY OF RESEARCH ADMINISTRATORS' GRANTSWEB

http://srainternational.com/cws/sra/resource.htm

Remember: All areas of government are interested in advancing the welfare of the population by promoting educational opportunities. Visit the Society of Research Administrators' (SRA) GrantsWeb site for easy access and funding information in four categories: Government Resources, Private Funding Resources, General Resources (including grant forms from a variety of agencies), and Policy Information and Regulations. Explore the Federal category carefully because links to funding opportunities abound. For example, Grant Opportunities Relevant to Rural Health are compiled under the U.S. Department of Agriculture's GRANTLINE.

Site Listings for the Department of Agriculture

Also found under the Department of Agriculture are Cooperative State Research, Education, and Extension Services (CSREES) Grants. These include:

- Fund for Rural America
- Higher Education Challenge Grants Program
- Higher Education Multicultural Scholars Program
- Tribal Colleges Extension Program
- Sustainable Agriculture Research and Education Program

Other Federal sources that may be of special interest to educators can be found at SRA's GrantsWeb. They include:

Site Listing for the National Institutes of Health

National Institutes of Health (NIH) offers excellent sources of grant information, such as:

- Frequently Asked Questions About Proposal Preparation
- MODULAR GRANTS PAGE
  — NIH Guide Notice (NIH Modular Grant Applications: Modifications and Update)
  — Important Modular Grant Information (web sites and contact listings)
  — Modular Applications and Awards (a Power Point slide presentation)

Offices Listed for the U.S. Department of Commerce

These include the following:

- National Oceanic and Atmospheric Administration
- National Telecommunications and Information Administration (grants and assistance)

Offices Listed for the U.S. Department of Energy

These include the following:

- Office of Energy Grants and Contracts
- DOE Federal Energy Technology Center
- DOE Financial Assistance
- DOE Pacific Northwest National Lab

Offices Listed for the U.S. Department of Justice

These include the following:

- Justice Grant Programs (from National Criminal Justice Reference Service)
- Office of Juvenile Justice and Delinquency Prevention—Grant & Funding Information
- National Institute of Justice—Grant Programs

Offices Listed for the U.S. Department of Transportation

These include the following:

- U.S. Electronic Grants Project
- Federal Aviation Administration—Office of Research and Technology Applications
- Federal Highway Administration

Offices Listed for the U.S. Department of State

These include the following:

- Fulbright Program
- Bureau of Educational and Cultural Affairs

Figure 4.1. National Science Foundation's FastLane System

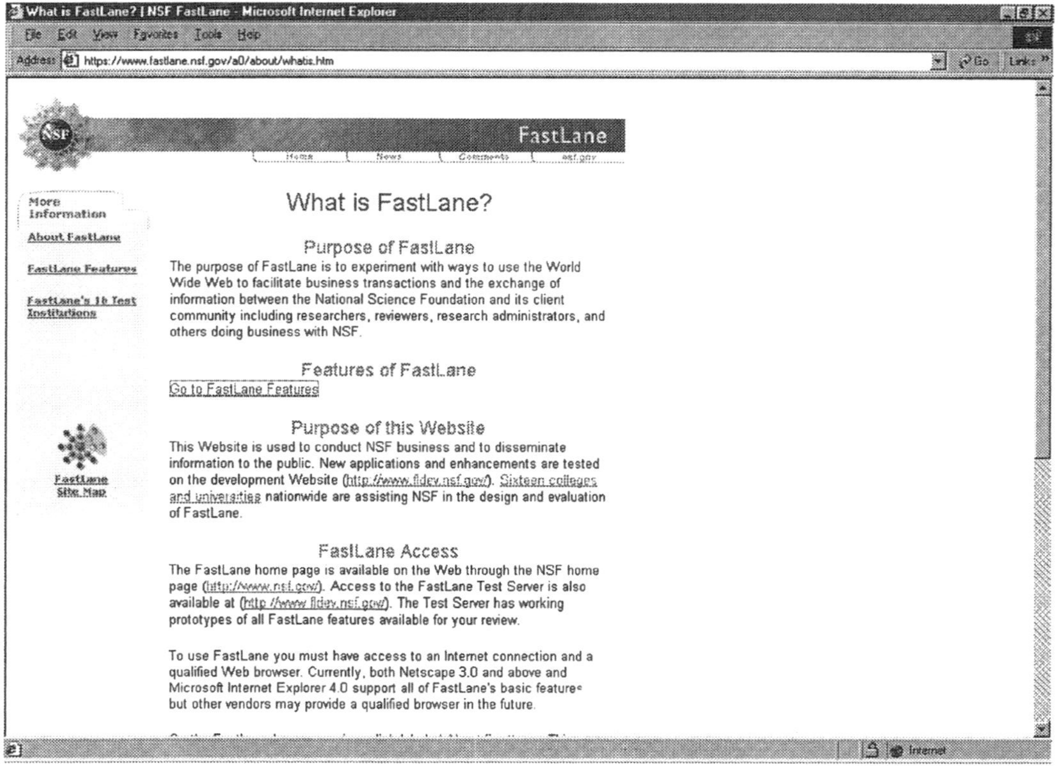

Other Federal Sites for Which Direct Links Are Given

Other federal programs have direct links to their own sites that provide excellent sources of information about grants and funding. For example,

- Institute of Museum and Library Services (http://www.imls.gov)
- National Endowment for the Humanities (http://www.neh.fed.us/)
- National Endowment for the Arts (http://arts.endow.gov/)
- Bureau of Educational and Cultural Affairs—offers links to Fulbright Programs and other cultural exchanges (http://exchanges.state.gov/)
- National Science Foundation (http://www.nsf.gov/)

The National Science Foundation's FastLane uses a variety of technology applications and features for online proposal preparation, proposal review, fellowship application, and travel information transfer. Presentations and workshops are conducted across the nation to assist in NSF proposal development and in using the FastLane system. Is FastLane the way funding agencies will be doing business in the future? Definitely! (See Figure 4.1 for a screenshot of the home page or go to http://www.fastlane.nsf. gov)

CONCLUSION

Remember to expand your search for education-related grants beyond the U.S. Department of Education! Gain a full understanding of the intents of our federal organizations and agencies. Utilize the free online government publications, the

Federal Register, and CFDA, and take time to learn the abbreviations and codes in order to use theim effectively. For example,

- *ED*—U.S. Department of Education
- *EPA*—Environmental Protection Agency
- *DOE*—U.S. Department of Energy
- *NARA*—National Archives and Records Administration
- *NEH*—National Endowment for the Humanities
- *NPS*—National Park Service
- *NSF*—National Science Foundation
- *SI*—Smithsonian Institution
- *USDA*—U.S. Department of Agriculture
- *USGS*—U.S. Geological Survey
- *WH*—White House

5

— ▸ ◂ —

All About Foundations

Are you aware that foundation giving in the United States
is approaching nearly $20 billion per year? What may be even
more surprising is that education ranks first in the number of
dollars received and second in the percentage of grants
awarded. Figure 5.1 provides a graphical representation of
this data.

Typically, most foundations do not fund individuals.
Foundation grants are primarily aimed at nonprofit, charitable
organizations certified by the Internal Revenue Service as
501(c)(3) public charities whose activities and programs match
those of a foundation's philanthropic priority areas. These
areas are most often categorized as charitable, educational, scientific, religious, literary, or cultural. Although many will consider providing general support, others prefer to fund specific
projects or activities, while rejecting other expenses, such as
salaries or building costs.

Figure 5.1. Education Maintained Its First-Place Rank by Share of Foundation Grant Dollars in 1998; Human Services Continued to Lead by Share of Grants

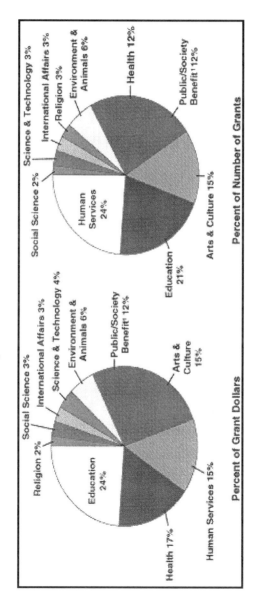

SOURCE: Foundation Giving Trends, The Foundation Center, 79 Fifth Avenue, New York, NY 10003-3076. (http://www.foundationcenter.org) Used by permission.

Note: Based on a sample of 1,009 larger foundations. Because of rounding, percentages may not total 100.
[1] Includes civil rights and social action, community improvement, philanthropy and voluntarism, and public affairs.

43

Public schools, libraries, and other government organizations may also qualify as public charities, although they usually have not applied for 501(c)(3) status. If a particular type of funding is dependent upon having 501(c)(3) status (call the foundation's contact person if there is a question) and your school does not qualify, consider partnering with a nonprofit organization in your community.

According to the Foundation Center, there are six different types of foundations:

Community foundation—A 501(c)(3) organization that makes grants for charitable purposes in a specific community or region.

Company-sponsored foundation—A private foundation whose assets are derived primarily from the contributions of a for-profit business; also referred to as a *corporate foundation*.

Family foundation: An independent, private foundation whose funds are derived from members of a single family.

General-purpose foundation: An independent, private foundation that awards grants in many different fields of interest.

Operating foundation: A 501(c)(3) organization classified by the IRS as a private foundation whose primary purpose is to conduct research, social welfare, or other programs determined by its governing body or establishment charter.

Special-purpose foundation: A private foundation that focuses its grantmaking activities in one or a few areas of interest.

THE FOUNDATION CENTER

http://www.foundationcenter.org/

To find out more than you ever wanted to know about the world of foundations, spend some time browsing the Foundation Center's Website. You'll find an easy to use, up-to-date site that contains a treasure trove of information. Of special interest to the novice grantwriter is the *Proposal Writing Course*, which is accessed from the Quick Links menu on the home page. This two-part course offers comprehensive tips on writing a proposal, including the rationale, budget, and evaluation. There are even tips on how to learn from rejection.

This independent, nonprofit information clearinghouse was established in 1956, and its publications, such as *The Foundation 1000*, *The Foundation Directory*, and *Guide to U.S. Foundations*, have been known to grantwriters for years (visit the Marketplace link to view the publications). Its mission is to foster public understanding of the foundation field by collecting, organizing, analyzing, and disseminating information on foundations, corporate giving, and related subjects. Headquartered in New York and with other offices in Washington, D.C., Atlanta, Cleveland, and San Francisco, their site is useful to grantseekers, grantmakers, researchers, policy makers, the media, and the general public.

The Foundation Center provides links to more than 1,000 foundation Websites. Click on "Grant Maker Info" on the Center's home page, and you'll find links that are organized in two ways: (a) by type—private foundation, corporate grantmakers, grantmaking public charities, or community foundations; and (b) by total assets and total-giving patterns of the top private foundations, corporate grantmakers, and community foundations.

Just how many dollars do foundations have in assets, and how much do they give in grants and awards? The information in Tables 5.1, 5.2, and 5.3 is excerpted from the Foundation Center's lists of Top 100 U. S. Foundations by total giving and

Table 5.1 Largest Grantmaking Foundations (Ranked by
Total Giving)

Foundation	Total giving ($)	Assets ($)
1. The Ford Foundation http://www.fordfound.org	440,400,415	9,675,452,326
2. Lilly Endowment Inc. (IN) (URL not available)	425,188,708	14,238,193,778
3. The Robert Wood Johnson Foundation (NJ) http://www.rwjf.org	289,143,569	7,867,784,532
4. The David and Lucile Packard Foundation (CA) http://www.packfound.org	263,929,118	9,577,894,120
5. W.K. Kellogg Foundation (MI) http://www.wkkf.org	202,919,594	6,387,840,996
6. The Pew Charitable Trusts (PA) http://www.pewtrusts.com	161,411,658	4,734,121,560
7. The New York Community Trust http://www.nycommunitytrust.org	144,912,318	1,759,019,641
8. The Andrew W. Mellon Foundation (NY) http://www.mellon.org	142,216,007	3,436,508,062
9. Open Society Institute (NY) http://www.soros.org/osi.html	124,623,703	n/a
10. John D. & Catherine T. MacArthur Foundation (IL) http://www.macfdn.org	123,517,237	4,168,672,836

by asset size. (Note: Data is procured from audited reports;
therefore, the amounts listed are not for the current year.)

Many of these corporations and foundations list education
as a main giving priority, but the focus may relate to a specific
area of education, such as urban education, literacy, or higher

Table 5.2 Top Three Largest Corporate Foundations Ranked by
Asset Size (from the Foundation Center's list of the Top
50 Corporate Grantmakers)

Name (State)	Total Assets	Total Giving in Dollars
1. Alcoa Foundation (PA) http://www.reeusda.gov/ pavnet/fd/fdalcoa.htm	$392,878,585	$16,665,883
2. Fannie Mae Foundation (DC) http://www. fanniemaefoundation.org	385,379,385	32,738,878
3. Norwest Foundation (MN)	307,349,934	16,180,448

education. It is typical for corporate foundations to offer programs only in areas where they have a corporate presence.

As previously stated, most foundations do not make
grants to individuals, although some have special award programs or scholarships. By visiting their sites, it is possible to
determine their main areas of funding interest, find out deadlines and geographic restrictions, and, in some instances,
download application forms.

In addition to providing general information about foundations, grantwriters will find the Foundation Center's specialized key word search and Search Zone features very helpful. By conducting a search for your city or state, you may
uncover foundations that you were not previously aware of
but that have funded programs near you. Matches can be
found for the following types of foundations:

- Private Foundations on the Internet
- Corporate Grantmakers
- Community Foundations
- Grantmaking Public Charities

Table 5.3 Largest Corporate Foundations Ranked by Total Giving

Name	Total Giving in Dollars
1. Bank of America Foundation http://www.bankofamerica.com/foundation/	$53,200,397
2. AT&T Foundation (NY) http://www.att.com/foundation/	46,066,194
3. The UPS Foundation (GA) http://www.community.ups.com/community/resources/foundation/index.html	42,723,327

The Center's RFP Bulletin

When visiting the Center's site, be sure to subscribe to the *RFP* (Request for Proposals) *Bulletin*, which is listed on the Quick Links (drop-down menu), and have RFPs delivered automatically to your e-mail address. These brief overviews of funding opportunities are published weekly in conjunction with the posting of *Philanthropy News Digest* to the Web. More detailed information can then be found by connecting to a grantmaker's Website or by contacting the grantmaker directly for complete program guidelines and eligibility requirements.

Foundation Center Libraries and Cooperating Collections

The Foundation Center's libraries, which operate in Atlanta, Cleveland, New York, San Francisco, and Washington, D.C., contain collections of materials on philanthropy. There, professional reference librarians are on hand to assist researchers in locating funding information by using Center publications, other materials, and electronic resources, including Internal Revenue Service 990-PF forms (returns filed by U.S. private foundations). Thanks to Internet capabilities, those who do not live near one of the five Foundation Center libraries can unearth a wealth of information about foundations, such as guidelines, personnel changes, or new grants in specific areas of interest. Although many Center resources and services are available on a complimentary basis, a fee is sometimes charged corresponding to the cost of online time or the amount of staff time required to fill a request.

Information about the Center's Cooperating Collections can also be found under the Quick Links (drop-down menu). These collections provide free access to funding information (which includes a core collection of Foundation Center publications) that can be found in libraries, community foundations, and other nonprofit resource centers across the country. To find the nearest collection to you, simply click on the link for your state. Collections marked with an asterisk have sets of private foundation information returns (IRS 990-PF forms) for their state, for neighboring states, or both. (Serious grantwriters find that researching 990-PF forms can help them to gauge the degree to which a foundation's previous record of giving matches their own need.) The core collection consists of the following:

- The Foundation Directory
- The Foundation Directory Part 2
- The Foundation Directory Supplement
- The Foundation 1000
- Foundation Fundamentals
- Foundation Giving
- The Foundation Grants Index
- The Foundation Grants Index Quarterly
- Foundation Grants to Individuals
- Guide to U.S. Foundations, Their Trustees, Officers, and Donors

- The Foundation Center's Guide to Proposal Writing
- National Directory of Corporate Giving
- National Guide to Funding (series)
- The Foundation Center's User-Friendly Guide.
- The Foundation Center's Guide to Grantseeking on the Web

Other Search Approaches

More comprehensive information about each foundation is provided by selecting "Top U.S. Funders" from the Quick Link list on the Center's home page. Most foundations have hyperlinks to their home pages. Because foundations tend to distribute funds in communities where they have a presence, it would be useful to search for sites of specific companies that operate in your community. The Foundation Center's search may help you to discover foundations that have funded projects in your geographic area from which you can generate targeted prospect lists.

If a corporate foundation does not have its own home page, funding information may be buried on the company's home page. Often, funding information can be located under such headers as *community involvement, site index,* or *other interests.* Most home pages do offer key word search capabilities within the site.

College and university home pages often provide excellent federal and state funding information that is usually accessible to the general public. Visit the home pages of colleges or universities in your state and look under such headings as *development* or *sponsored programs.*

For-Fee Services

If you still have questions, a relatively new addition to the Foundation Center's site is the assistance of an online librarian to answer questions about foundation grants and funding. The fee depends upon the complexity of the inquiry.

The Foundation Center also offers free and for-fee workshops on grantwriting and accessing library resources, and the five Foundation libraries provide overviews of the foundation and corporation funding research process.

If you feel the need for more information about foundations, you might consider subscribing to the *Foundation Directory Online* for $19.95 per month or $195 a year. You can generate targeted lists of funding prospects from among more than 10,000 of the nation's largest foundations. The Foundation Center's newest offering, *Foundation Directory Online Plus*, leads to even more sources of funding and features a searchable grants file with more than 100,000 grants awarded by the top grant givers in the nation. This service is available for $29.95 per month or $295 per year.

OTHER LAUNCH SITES
TO FOUNDATIONS

Rather than list names and addresses of specific foundations, the following serve as launch sites to home pages that offer impressive listings or links to funding sources, including foundations that have specific interests in education.

Pitsco

http://www.pitsco.com

From their home page, go to Resources for Educators, then click on Grants and Funding. Pitsco offers an impressive list of foundations, government sites, business, technology, and other funding resources. Be sure to check out the Educational Grant Sponsors Index, which provides links to numerous foundations that are interested in funding educational pro-

---

Box 5.1

In response to dwindling revenue, many school districts across America are establishing their own educational foundations. Regulations and costs of initiating a nonprofit organization vary by state. Lawyers will sometimes provide pro bono service to assist in such endeavors.

In a 1997 *Philanthropy News Digest* article, it was reported that Illinois educational foundations increased in number in the 1990s from 25 to 150. And in California, the number more than doubled in the 1985-1995 decade, from 204 to 537. The aim of this type of special interest foundation is usually to extend funding appeals to corporations and wealthy individuals.

Part VII of the Texas Education Agency's *A Grantseeker's Resource Guide to Obtaining Federal, Corporate, and Foundation Grants* (http://www.tea.state.tx.us/grant/) discusses how some school districts in Texas have started foundations or organizations whose sole purpose is to secure funding for the schools in their district by researching and submitting grant proposals.

---

jects. Math and science teachers especially will enjoy exploring this site.

Philanthropy News Network Online

http://pnnonline.org

Click on Links in the left index. Some corporations with an unexpected foundation presence, such as Ben and Jerry's, Adobe, and Autodesk can be found here.

Foundations Online

http://www.foundations.org/grantmakers.html

Go to this site, sponsored by the Northern California Community Foundation, Inc., and click on Directories to find foundations and grantmakers by name. You can scroll through the directory and click on a link to jump to a specific home page. Note: Access to some foundations on the previous page are offered as a link to home pages residing on other servers.

*Non-Government Funding
Information Resources*

http://www.amherst.edu/~develop/resources/
resonlin/intsource.html

The Non-Government Funding Information Resources site was created by the development office at Amherst College. It offers several unusual links for the researcher and academician.

The Community Resource Institute

http://www.granted.org/

This organization, based in Topeka, Kansas, aspires to become one of the most useful grant resource sites on the Internet. You can search foundations and other grant programs by specifying type of funding sources (nationwide, local, or corporate) or by grant category—Arts & Culture Grant Foundations, Community Development/Services Grant Foundations, Environmental Grant Foundations, Health Grant Foundations, Youth Grant Foundations, and Educational Grant Foundations. Currently, there are more than 100 foundations listed in the educational category.

CONCLUSION

The Foundation Center, established in 1956, fosters public understanding of the foundation field. Grantseekers, grantmakers, researchers, policy makers, the media, and the general public all make use of its resources; it is a virtual gold mine of information for both the novice and experienced grantwriter.

Novice grantwriters will enjoy browsing the frequently asked questions (FAQs), reading *A Proposal Writing Short Course*, viewing the glossary, and reviewing sample grant applications. Experienced grantwriters can make use of detailed information about funders or have specific questions answered by an online librarian. By using resources of the Foundation Center and other sites that link to foundations, you can research the foundations that operate in your community and generate a targeted list of prospects.

By subscribing to Foundation Center's *RFP Bulletin* or other lists, such as *Grantseeker Tips* (Chapter 10), you will be reminded often of newly developed grant sites and recently announced requests for proposals from private, corporate, and government sources.

6

Numbers, Numbers
Everywhere:
Other Useful Sites

Grantwriters always need to develop a purpose or problem statement. In other words, the purpose of the grant (or of
your receiving funding) is to address a specific need—that
is the reason for the proposal. The problem or need statement should be research based, and it should show evidence
of your knowledge of the extent of the problem in order to jus-
tify to the reader why the grant should be awarded. Statistics
provided by authoritative sources, literature reviews, or data
that is compiled as part of a self-study or needs assessment
will all support your needs statement or rationale. To this
end, the following sites may be of assistance in providing such
information.

U.S. CENSUS BUREAU

http://www.Census.gov

Serious grantwriters should take some time to acquaint
themselves with the many resources available at the U.S.

Figure 6.1. U.S. Census Bureau Website, Providing Demographic Information

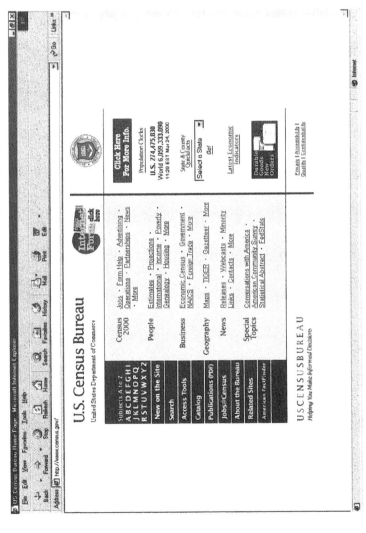

Census Bureau. Billed as a "source for social, demographic, and economic information," the Census Bureau has valuable data that most grantwriters will find quite useful because funders often require demographic information about the population served or the geographic area of service.

By visiting the Census Bureau (see Figure 6.1) and clicking on Search, voluminous amounts of information can be found about specific cities, counties, or states. In addition to population, county profile data can provide researchers with statistics on education levels, labor force, retail sales, or language spoken in the home. Many state and federal grants ask for congressional district information on the application. This information can also be easily retrieved through the word, place, or map search techniques available to the user.

The TIGER Map Service (found as a link on the home page or by clicking on the Access Tools button) is another project sponsored by the U.S. Bureau of the Census. The goal of this service is to provide a public resource for generating high-quality, detailed maps of sites in the United States. Veteran grantwriters know that including maps or other visuals can often provide a better means of reporting comparative or descriptive data than text alone. If you need a detailed map to illustrate a concept for your proposal, try using the TIGER Map Service.

SOCIAL STATISTICS BRIEFING ROOM

http://www.whitehouse.gov/fsbr/ssbr.html

The Social Statistics Briefing Room (SSBR) provides links to information produced by a number of federal agencies. All of the information included in the SSBR is maintained and updated by the statistical units of those agencies. You can find information on crime, demographics, education, and health statistics.

THE FEDERAL INTERAGENCY COUNCIL ON STATISTICAL POLICY

http://www.fedstats.gov/

An even more powerful site for locating statistical information collected by the government is the Federal Interagency Council on Statistical Policy, also known as FedStats. Here, you can access information from more than 70 government agencies by using either an alphabetic index or keyword search. For example, a search for *children AND violence* yielded 233 documents, including Bureau of Justice Department reports titled, "Violence-Related Injuries Treated in Hospital Emergency Departments" and "Trends in Juvenile Violence."

THE NATIONAL CENTER FOR EDUCATION STATISTICS

http://nces.ed.gov/

The National Center for Education Statistics (NCES) is the primary federal agency responsible for the collection, analysis, and reporting of data related to education in the United States. The five principal responsibilities of this agency are the following:

1. Make the data collected on education available to the public

2. Provide indicators on the status and trends in education

3. Report on the condition of education to Congress, state policy makers, educational practitioners, the media, the public, and users, such as you

4. Assist states and school districts in improving their statistical systems

5. Review and report on education in other nations

These data collections provide a unique resource to the grantwriter who is searching for primary data that can be used to corroborate the need to fund programs to improve the achievement levels of a specific population.

The NCES database contains information on the results of the *National Assessment of Educational Progress* (NAEP), also known as the *Nation's Report Card*. Since its inception in 1969, NAEP has periodically assessed students in Grades 4, 8, and 12 in numerous academic subjects, including mathematics, science, reading, writing, world geography, U.S. history, civics, social studies, and the arts. (In 1997, a small-scale assessment of visual arts, music, and dance was conducted.) Student test results are reported nationally, state by state, and by special interest areas (history, reading, etc.).

Although the NAEP is best known as an indicator of elementary and secondary student achievement, it also contains valuable information and results on two other components, the "School Characteristics and Policy Survey" and the "Teacher Survey," areas that may be of interest to those writing grants relating to professional development, teacher recruitment or preparation, education reform, policy development, or all of the above.

Other studies contained in the NCES files that may be useful to grantwriters include the following:

The Condition of Education, 1998 Edition. An annual report that focuses on 60 indicators, representing a consensus of professional judgment on the most significant national measures of the condition and progress of education. This is available in HTML and PDF format at http://nces.ed.gov/pubsearch/pubsinfo.asp?pubid = 98013.

Federal Support for Education: Fiscal Years 1980 to 1998. Provides a comprehensive picture of total federal financial support for education since fiscal year 1980. Http://nces. ed.gov/pubsearch/pubsinfo.asp?pubid = 98115.

School Policies and Practices Affecting Instruction in Mathematics. Focuses on who teaches math, reports the emphasis math instruction receives in the schools, and provides resources available in schools that support math learning. The Website is at http://nces.ed.gov/pubsearch/pubsinfo.asp? pubid = 98495.

Indicators of School Crime & Safety, 1998. First in a series of annual reports on school crime and safety from the Bureau of Justice Statistics and NCES. Their Website URL is http://nces.ed.gov/pubsearch/pubsinfo.asp?pubid = 98251.

Students Learning Science. Presents results relating to teachers' academic preparation and professional development, the amount of emphasis science instruction receives in schools, student course taking, and the availability of school resources that support science instruction. See their Website at http://nces.ed.gov/pubsearch/pubsinfo.asp?pubid = 98493.

State Comparisons of Education Statistics: 1969-70 to 1996-97. Holdings contain a compendium of state-level elementary, secondary, and higher education statistics. See http://nces.ed.gov/pubsearch/pubsinfo.asp?pubid = 98018.

REGIONAL EDUCATIONAL LABORATORIES NETWORK

http://www.relnetwork.org

Ever heard the term *regional education laboratory* (REL)? The U.S. Department of Education supports 10 of them. Each assists educators and policy makers in tackling state and local education challenges and in pursuing comprehensive school improvement strategies. These laboratories, which are supported by the U. S. Department of Education, Office of Educational Research and Improvement, serve geographic regions that span the nation and work to assure that educators and others have access to the best available information from research and practice. Although each has a different focus, they work to assist educators with the following:

- Conducting development and applied research resulting in models for implementing systemic reform and for achieving improvement on a broad scale
- Providing information, training, and technical assistance to help states, schools, and communities to implement comprehensive school improvement strategies
- Promoting widespread access to information regarding research and best practice
- Creating communities of learners who collaborate with the laboratory in development and dissemination
- Cooperating with other agencies and programs to deliver services that support the efforts of educators and policy makers to improve education
- Forging strong links to the research community to promote the creation of new knowledge to improve education

The regional laboratories are as follows:

1. Appalachia Educational Laboratory (AEL)
http://www.ael.org
Specialty area: Rural education
Region served: Kentucky, Tennessee, Virginia, and West Virginia

2. Laboratory for Student Success (LSS; also known as
The Mid-Atlantic Regional Educational Laboratory)
http://www.temple.edu/departments/LSS
Specialty area: Urban education and urban education reform
Region served: Delaware, Maryland, New Jersey, Pennsylvania,
 and Washington, D.C.

3. Mid-Continent Research for Education and
Learning (McREL)
http://www.mcrel.org
Specialty area: Curriculum, learning, and instruction
Region served: Colorado, Kansas, Missouri, Nebraska, North
Dakota, South Dakota, and Wyoming

4. North Central Regional Educational Laboratory (NCREL)
http://www.ncrel.org
Specialty area: Educational technology
Region served: Illinois, Indiana, Iowa, Michigan, Minnesota,
Ohio, and Wisconsin

5. Northeast and Islands Regional Educational Laboratory at
Brown University (LAB at Brown University)
http://www.lab.brown.edu
Specialty area: Language and cultural diversity
Region served: Connecticut, Maine, Massachusetts, New
Hampshire, New York, Rhode Island, Vermont, Puerto Rico,
and the Virgin Islands

6. Northwest Regional Educational Laboratory (NWREL)
http://www.nwrel.org
Specialty area: School change processes
Region served: Alaska, Idaho, Montana, Oregon, and
Washington

7. Pacific Resources For Education and Learning (PREL)
http://www.prel.org

Specialty area: Language and cultural diversity
Region served: American Samoa, the Commonwealth of the Northern Mariana Islands, the Federated States of Micronesia, Guam, Hawaii, the Republic of the Marshall Islands, and the Republic of Palau

8. SERVE
http://www.serve.org
Specialty area: Early childhood education
Region served: Alabama, Florida, Georgia, Mississippi, North Carolina, and South Carolina

9. Southwest Educational Development Laboratory (SEDL)
http://www.sedl.org
Specialty area: Language and cultural diversity
Region served: Arkansas, Louisiana, New Mexico, Oklahoma, and Texas

10. WestEd
http://www.wested.org
Specialty area: Assessment and accountability
Region served: Arizona, California, Nevada, and Utah

EDUCATIONAL RESOURCES INFORMATION CENTER

http://www.accesseric.org

A part of the U.S. Department of Education's National Library System, the Educational Resources Information Center (ERIC) recently celebrated 30 years of providing education-related materials and research to the public. As the world's largest and most frequented education database, ERIC can be used to locate information on any topic related to education. Just a few years ago, most educational researchers would spend hours at a library poring over the ERIC index to identify the microfiche to access information found in ERIC. Now the Internet, with its easy access and search capabilities, is justifiably gaining popularity. Although some ERIC articles and documents need to be accessed via microfiche (or ordered on the Internet through the ERIC service), the process of conducting a search is now easier and much less time-consuming, thanks to the Internet.

Because ERIC is so large (there are 16 clearinghouses, 10 adjunct clearinghouses, and additional support components), a good starting point is the system-wide Website listed earlier. At this site, there is an overview of the ERIC system and links to its components. You can search the database and print or download copies of the more than 1,600 ERIC digests from here also. Read the FAQs (frequently asked questions) to find out how to access full-text ERIC articles.

Probably the best-known ERIC site is AskERIC at http://ericir.syr.edu, which features a virtual library including hundreds of lesson plans and InfoGuides that can help pull together topics on a variety of educational issues, such as school reform, site-based management, parent programs, and community collaboration.

CONSUMER INFORMATION CENTER

http://www.pueblo.gsa.gov/

Do you need to purchase inexpensive informational materials or pamphlets for the clientele being served in a grant? Consider "shopping" at the Consumer Information Center!

Millions of Americans have written to the Consumer Information Center (CIC) in Pueblo, Colorado, for government publications. Established in 1970 as a separately funded operation within the U.S. General Services Administration, the CIC helps federal agencies and departments develop and distribute useful information to the public.

Grantwriters whose interest lies in parenting, health or nutrition, economics, or adult education will find many pamphlets (some in Spanish) that can be used either for instruction or general dissemination, such as "Schools Without Drugs" and "Helping Your Child Become a Reader." Although you can download and print many of the documents directly from your computer, ordering documents in large quantities is usually less expensive than making your own copies. (Remember, this is a government service, and the costs have been underwritten by taxpayers.)

Individuals who review grants carefully screen proposed budgets to see that money is being spent wisely. Rarely can your grant dollars go farther than when buying printed products through the CIC.

UNIVERSAL SERVICE ADMINISTRATIVE COMPANY

http://www.universalservice.org

The Universal Service Administrative Company (USAC) is the private, nonprofit organization responsible for providing schools, libraries, and rural health care providers in the United States with affordable telecommunications services through the E-rate program. E-rate provides discounts on telecommunications services, Internet access, and internal connections to libraries and schools. Discounts range from 20% to 90% and are based on the poverty level in the local community.

By clicking on the Schools and Libraries Program link from the USAC home page, you can find an overview of program information and step-by-step online application procedures for E-rate funding.

MICKEY'S PLACE IN THE SUN

http://people.delphi.com/mickjyoung/index.html

Plan on spending a lot of time at Mickey's Place in the Sun. The name may sound frivolous, but this is a very informative, seriously useful site with links to social work and social services resources that include clearinghouses, organizations, policy and research, programs and strategies, publications, statistics, and universities and colleges. The site will appeal to educators, students, policy makers, media, law enforcement personnel, community leaders, businesses, religious leaders, advocates, and service providers because there are vast selections of links for each area. Grantwriters will find useful links to funding sources (arranged by topic), statistics, educational resources, and numerous other topics.

BUROS INSTITUTE OF MENTAL MEASUREMENT

http://www.unl.edu/buros

Grantwriters often need to compile a data-gathering instrument or use an existing one. To find out whether an appropriate instrument already exists, visit the Buros Institute of Mental Measurement. Buros publishes the *Mental Measurements Yearbook, Tests in Print,* and the *Buros Desk Reference Series.* Researchers can find information on the purpose, statistical characteristics, and, when available, the norms for most tests. The site includes links to test reviews, test publishers, and test files.

THE EDUCATIONAL TESTING SERVICE NETWORK

http://www.ets.org

The Educational Testing Service Network, based in Princeton, New Jersey, offers information on standardized tests and research instruments. The site is very comprehensive and offers a tests and services directory. The Online Store features one-stop shopping for educational products, software, and publications. Browse the Test Prep Products link to find specific measurement instruments that may assist in collecting appropriate data for your program.

THE INTERNET PUBLIC LIBRARY
REFERENCE QUOTATIONS

http://www.ipl.org/ref/RR/static/ref5500.html

Some grantwriters like to use a quotation to introduce or summarize an important topic. Finding just the right quote can be accomplished easily by using the Internet. From Bart Simpson to Bartlett, thousands of quotations can be searched in just seconds. The Internet Public Library (IPL) Ready Reference Collection can help identify or find interesting quotations.

UNIVERSITY OF VIRGINIA
INTERNET REFERENCE SOURCES

http://www.lib.virginia.edu/reference/

Grantwriters will find this site extremely useful. Included here are dictionaries, encyclopedias, quotations, statistics, maps, and opinion polls. The Grants link currently provides access to the Sponsored Programs Information Network, or SPIN. This powerful program allows the user to search for grants by keyword, geographical location, sponsor, deadline dates, and more. Entering the descriptors can be time-consuming but is well worth it.

VASSARSTAT

http://faculty.vassar.edu/~lowry/VassarStats.html

VassarStat, according to author Richard Lowry, Professor of Psychology at Vassar College, provides "a useful and user-friendly tool for performing basic statistical computation." For those grant evaluators whose programs or projects call for such statistical procedures as correlation or regression analysis, ANOVA, *t*-tests, and ANCOVA, this site provides explanations for using various procedures and easy data entry capabilities.

CONCLUSION

As experienced grantwriters know, stating a need is one of the most important components of a grant. It is essential to write a well-developed, research-based statement of need for your proposed project, and the Internet can provide resources that will locate statistics, maps, comparative data, and other useful demographic information. Sites such as ERIC can provide educators with research findings or information on what is working in other school districts or classrooms across the country. Inexpensive, printed resources that are useful to educators working with children or adults can be located at the CIC.

7

———◆◆———

Make the Most
of What You've Got

Educational Organizations and Associations

Are you a member of a state or national educational association or organization? If so, consider visiting your association's home page to determine whether there may be dollars available for you! Many organizations offer special grants, awards, stipends, or fellowships for members only. Such funding opportunities offer the distinct advantage of limiting the number of applicants, thereby narrowing the pool of competitors.

Most subject-oriented educational organization home pages contain attractive links to curriculum information, teaching ideas, or activities. Do not overlook the Member Services link (sometimes referred to as Member Benefits or Constituent Relations), where you can find information about awards and competitive programs. (If all else fails, there should be a Search option within the site.) If you are a dues-paying member of an educational group, the chances are very good that you (or your students) will qualify to apply for special fellowships, awards, and grants through the organization. The following organizations provide good examples of these principles.

PHI DELTA KAPPA

http://www.pdkintl.org

Phi Delta Kappa's (PDK) Website contains information on PDK-sponsored travel seminars. Current visits are planned for Europe and Asia. Although nonmembers may participate in the seminars, only PDK members are eligible to receive the Gerald Howard Read International Seminar Scholarships. The Educational Foundation has a link to information on the following grants and fellowships that help to achieve PDK's goals:

- Scholarship Grants for Prospective Educators
- Summer Camp/Institute For Prospective Teachers
- Phi Delta Kappa International Graduate Fellowships In Educational Leadership
- Victoria C. T. Read Adopt-A-Scholar and Scholarship Program
- Excellence in Student Teaching Awards

NATIONAL EDUCATION ASSOCIATION'S NFIE GRANTS

(National Foundation for the Improvement of Education)

http://www.nfie.org

In 1969, the National Education Association created the National Foundation for the Improvement of Education, which provides grants and technical assistance to teachers, education support personnel, and higher education faculty and staff to improve student learning in the nation's public schools. This operating foundation also funds programs for teams of educators working in, or on behalf of, America's public schools. The basic goal of NFIE is to improve student achievement by providing educators with opportunities to engage in high-quality professional development.

NFIE targets the following categories:

- Dropout Prevention Strategies
- Christa McAuliffe Educators and Fellows
- $1,000 Leadership Grants (to enhance professional growth)
- Teaching and Technology (to improve teaching and learning)

THE ASSOCIATION OF SUPERVISION AND CURRICULUM DEVELOPMENT

http://www.ascd.org

To locate the latest grant information at ASCD Web, click on the Search button and submit the word *grant*. Here you can find information such as the summary, "Designing Successful Grant Proposals."

NATIONAL SCIENCE TEACHERS ASSOCIATION

http://www.nsta.org

The National Science Teachers Association (NSTA) offers more than 20 links to specific science awards and competitions of interest to K-12 science teachers and students. What better way to encourage and motivate students than to engage them in student competitions that offer monetary prizes and other recognition to individuals or student teams? For example, the Toshiba ExploraVision Awards Program encourages teams of students to explore the research and development of new technology. Winning teams, such as those that envisioned "SMAART: Shape Memory Alloys in Airplanes Reduce Turbulence" or knee replacements that grow inside the kneecap, receive $500. Another is the Duracell Competition, which awards $100,000 in bonds to student inventors. The NSTA site provides direct access to many of the entry forms. The site also has information on teacher award programs, such as the Science Teaching Award and the Distinguished Service to Science Education Award.

INTERNATIONAL READING ASSOCIATION

http://www.reading.org

The International Reading Association (IRA) has information about the following grants and awards, some of which are available to members only:

- Children's Literature Awards
- Council Service Awards
- Dissertation Awards and Grants
- International Reading Association Literacy Award
- Media Awards
- Professional Development Awards and Grants
- Research Awards and Grants
- Service Awards
- Teachers' Awards and Grants

Members of the IRA should check with state and local councils for additional opportunities.

NATIONAL COUNCIL FOR TEACHERS OF ENGLISH

http://www.ncte.org

The National Council for Teachers of English offers Achievement Awards in Writing, the Promising Young Writers Program for Eighth-Grade Students, a Grants-in-Aid Program, and a Teacher-Researcher grant.

THE AMERICAN ASSOCIATION OF SCHOOL ADMINISTRATORS

http://www.aasa.org

The American Association of School Administrators (AASA) offers one of the best maintained, up-to-date, and informative grant and funding sites available. Go to http://www.aasa.org/ Issues/grants/grants.htm. Numerous links exist there that provide information of interest to school administrators and teachers alike. Among them are

- OJJDP (Office of Juvenile Justice and Delinquency Prevention) programs

- Telecommunications and Information Infrastructure Assistance Program

- Technology Innovation Challenge Grants

- Comprehensive School Reform Demonstration Program
- Sources of Federal Support for Educational Technology
- U.S. Department of Agriculture Rural Utilities Service
- Grant opportunities from the Department of Education

AASA's site also offers springboards to other links that provide information on technology support for schools. Found at http://www.aasa.org/Issues/Grants/techgrants.htm, this list of educational technology resources includes the following:

- American Library Association (http://www.ala.org)
- Consortium for School Networking (http://www.cosn.org)
- Department of Education Technology Page (http://www. ed.gov/Technology/)
- Education and Library Networks Coalition (http://www.itc.org/edlinc)
- Educause Home Page (http://www.educause.edu/)
- EDWeb (http://edweb.gsn.org)
- ERIC Clearinghouse on Information and Technology (ERIC/CIT) (http://ericir.syr.edu/ithome/)
- Global SchoolNet Foundation (http://www.gsn.org)
- LearnNet (http://www.fcc.gov/learnnet/)
- National Academy of Sciences (http://www.nas.edu/nap/online/techgap)
- National Center for Technology Planning (http://www.nctp.com)
- Pathways to School Improvement (http://www.ncrel.org/ncrel/sdrs/pathwayg.htm.)
- Regional Technology in Education Consortia (R*TEC) (http://rtec.org/)
- Web66: A K12 World Wide Web (http://Web66.coled.umn.edu)

NATIONAL ART EDUCATION FOUNDATION

http://www.naea-reston.org/programs

The National Art Education Foundation (NAEF), sister organization to the National Art Education Association, currently administers four programs:

1. Teacher Incentive Program Projects promote the teaching of art.
2. The Mary McMullan Fund Projects promote art education as an integral part of the curriculum and seek to improve art instruction in public and private K-12 schools and higher education.
3. The NAEA Research Fund endorses the Association's efforts to initiate and encourage research in art education.
4. The Ruth Halvorsen Professional Development Fund Scholarships promote the use of the goals for student learning as communicated through the Visual Arts Standards.

Scholarships are awarded to NAEA members.

COUNCIL FOR EXCEPTIONAL CHILDREN

http://www.cec.sped.org/

The Council for Exceptional Children (CEC) is the largest international professional organization dedicated to improving educational outcomes for individuals with exceptionalities (disabilities or giftedness). The CEC Foundation offers scholarship awards for college-bound students and offers minigrants for special educators.

NEW-TEACHER.COM

http://www.new-teacher.com

If a professional organization has not been listed earlier in this chapter, you may want to visit the home page of New-Teacher.com. The "Being a Professional" link (left index) will lead to a link for a list of national, multidisciplined, professional educational organizations.

CONCLUSION

If you have invested money to be a member of a professional organization, find out whether you may be able to reap some of the benefits! Don't overlook state and local affiliates of national organizations either. If you are not a member of an educational organization, it may be worthwhile to do some research and join one that has opportunities for members that are closely aligned with your areas of interest.

Box 7.1

The *.org* ending on the addresses for educational associations denotes the address of a nonprofit organization, usually one with an IRS 501(c)(3) designation. Many, but not all, educational organizations use their organization's abbreviation followed by *.org* as their URL. Organizations routinely publish these addresses on promotional materials or publications. Using a search engine (see Chapter 2) is also an option for locating the address of an educational organization.

8

---•◄—

Read All About It!

Online Book Sellers,
Journals, and Publishing Companies

Although just about any type of information can be found online, some people would prefer a printed format for learning about writing grants or locating grant resources. Once again, you can turn to the Internet!

ONLINE BOOK SELLERS

An early leader in online book sales was Amazon.com. Formerly land-only bookstores have also followed suit, including Barnes & Noble and Borders. A new development to some book sales sites has been the addition of music compact discs and software materials. You can find the major online booksellers at the following URLs:

- Amazon.com   http://www.amazon.com
- Barnes & Noble.com http://www.barnesandnoble.com
- Borders.com   http://www.Borders.com

Using online booksellers can assist grantwriters in a number of ways. For example,

- You write a successful grant for staff development on "grantwriting," and now must purchase printed materials for your school's professional library
- You want to become aware of recent publications on a given topic
- You need to research a topic, and want to know who the leading authors are
- You want to locate the latest edition of a publication or find out what else an author has published
- You know the name of a book but need its International Standard Book Number (ISBN) to order it or find its cost
- You are developing a budget for a family literacy program and need to list possible items for purchase
- You need to find out what books are appropriate for various age or grade levels

The process of visiting an online bookstore and performing a search for books about grantwriting will yield a surprising number of publications, some of which are very specific to certain fields, including education. At these sites, you can perform a book search by title, author, or subject. Some sample titles found at the Borders.com, Amazon.com, and Barnes & Noble.com sites that may be of interest to educators who are interested in writing grants include the following, given along with their list prices and ISBNs:

Get a Grant, Yes You Can
Norris, Dennis (1998)
$8.95 (ISBN 0590963872)

Grant Application Writer's Handbook
Reif-Lehrer, Liane (1995)
$40.00 (ISBN 0867208740)

Grant Proposals: A Primer for Writers
Mathis, Emily D.; Doody, John E. (1994)
$7.85 (ISBN 1558331298)

The Principal's Guide to Winning Grants
Bauer, David G. (1999)
$24.95 (ISBN 0787944947)

Proposals That Work: A Guide for Planning Dissertations and Grant Proposals
Locke, Lawrence F.; Silverman, Stephen J.; Spirduso, Waneen W. (1999)
$29.95 (ISBN 0761917071)

The Teacher's Guide to Winning Grants
Bauer, David G. (1998)
$24.95 (ISBN 0787944939)

Designing Successful Grant Proposals
Orlich, Donald C. (1996)
$20.95 (ISBN 0871202646)

Effective Grant Writing: Schools, Social Service Agencies, Nonprofit Organizations
Williams, Karen N.; Moore, Darryl (1998)
$24.95 (ISBN 0966440609)

From Idea to Funded Project: Grant Proposals That Work
Belcher, Jane C.; Jacobsen, Julia M. (1992)
$32.50 (ISBN 0897747100)

Grant Proposal Writing: A Handbook for School Library Media Specialists
Woolls, Blanche (1986)
$42.95 (ISBN 0313244405)

Grant Writing Basics (pamphlet)
Morrell, Jessica P. (1996)
$7.50 (ISBN 1884241395)

Grant Writing for Teachers: If You Can Write a Lesson Plan
You Can Write a Grant
Karges-Bone, Linda; Heggie, Tom (1994)
$14.99 (ISBN 0866538232)

Grassroots Grants: An Activist's Guide to Proposal Writing
Robinson, Andy; Klein, Kim (1996)
$25.00 (ISBN 096202225X)

Pocket Guide to Grant Applications
Crombie, Iain K.; Du V Florey, Charles (1999)
$29.95 (ISBN 0727912194)

Recipe for Grant Writing: A Simplistic Guide for Schools, Religious,
& Community Agencies
Freeman, Algeania (1997)
$15.00 (ISBN 1575024845)

Six Easy Steps to Millions in Grants: A Grant-Writing Manual
Winn, Debra M. (1993)
$24.90 (ISBN 0963848003)

Other publications related to education can also be located at online bookstores and may be useful in developing your proposal's narrative. Consider, for example, searching for such terms as the following:

- Teacher effectiveness
- Methods of instruction and study
- Teacher training and development
- Teaching methods and materials
- Education reform
- Technology and education

ONLINE JOURNALS

Education Week

http://www.edweek.org

Teacher Magazine

http://www.edweek.org/tm/
OR
http://www.teachermagazine.org

Educators may already be familiar with the printed versions of *Education Week* and *Teacher Magazine*. Both can now be accessed on the Internet at http://www.edweek.org. Because *Education Week* maintains such current information, it is useful to peruse the online headlines regularly for items of interest. For example, the January 12, 2000, issue contained an article on the newly launched foundation of the Goldman Sachs Group Inc., which pledged to award $10 million in grants to education worldwide during the 1999-2000 school year.

The online versions of educational journals include many of the same news articles as the printed versions and can be very useful when collecting information and current data for writing grants. Currently, there is no charge for accessing the archives and performing a keyword search.

A most impressive compilation of grants that are of interest to K-12 teachers can be found under Grants and Fellowships at *Teacher Magazine*! Grants, contests, awards, and other deadlines can all be found there. The 10 grants and fellowships available to individuals and schools that were listed online in the February 2000 issue of *Teacher Magazine* included the following:

1. The Earthwatch Teacher Fellowship, which offers educators opportunities to participate in 2-week expeditions throughout the world during the summer of 2000.

2. The National Foundation for the Improvement of Education Leadership Grants for Educators. Up to fifty $1,000 grants are awarded.

3. The National Geographic Society Education Foundation grants that support innovative geography education. Approximately 30 grants of up to $1,250 each are awarded.

4. Schools, colleges, museums, and other nonprofit organizations may apply for the Humanities Focus Grant offered by the National Endowment for the Humanities. The maximum award is $25,000 and covers the cost of travel, materials, and administration.

5. Curriculum Associates presents grants to K-8 teachers who make effective use of teaching tools such as technology and print. Three educators each receive $1,000, plus a $500 gift certificate for Curriculum Associates materials.

The Chronicle of Higher Education:
Academe This Week

http://www.chronicle.com

Known primarily to higher education personnel in its printed format, the *Chronicle of Higher Education* is now available online. Many of the grants, fellowships, and other awards listed in this publication are suitable for all levels of education as well. However, only individuals who subscribe to its printed version may apply for a user name and password to access current grants and announcements online. A collection of previous grants that have been awarded to colleges and universities for the past 5 years is also available here.

The Chronicle of Philanthropy

http://www.philanthropy.com/

Administrators of educational foundations or educators who volunteer on boards of nonprofit organizations may find *The Chronicle of Philanthropy* helpful. This journal addresses such topics as corporate funding allocations, fundraising techniques, nonprofit employment opportunities, and foundation management (including IRS regulations, etc.). Subscription service is available to *The Chronicle Guide to Grants*, which is an electronic data base of all corporate and foundation grants listed in *The Chronicle of Philanthropy* since 1995.

ARTSEDGE NewsBreak

**http://www.artsedge.kennedy-center.org/
newsbreak/artsedge.cfm**

Administered by the Kennedy Center's Education Department, this online publication highlights newsworthy information and developments in the area of arts education, including links to the arts education community, news headlines, arts and education events, funding, competitions, and conferences. The ARTSEDGE home page (http://artsedge.kennedy-center. org) also has links to other sites useful to humanities teachers.

Early Childhood News

http://www.earlychildhood.com

This publication is a resource for childcare professionals who work with young children, birth to age 6. You can also find information about online professional development activities for continuing credit.

Classroom Connect!

http://www.classroom.net/home.asp

This online publication bills itself as the home base on the Internet for education-related resources, products, information, and support. Information about technology conferences; online courses provided by Connected University, Classroom Connect's accredited professional development program; and online learning adventures for students can be found here.

ONLINE PUBLISHING COMPANIES

Corwin Press

http://www.corwinpress.com

Books and other publications can often be purchased online from the publisher's website. Corwin Press specializes in books for educators that are based on theory, research, practical experience, or all of the above. Educators who are interested in writing grants may want to consider these titles offered by Corwin Press:

*Finding Funding: Grantwriting From Start to Finish,
Including Project Management and Internet Use* (3rd ed.).

Brewer, Ernest W.; Achilles, Charles M.; Fuhriman, Jay R.
$49.95(ISBN 0803966814)

Funding Special Education
Parrish, Thomas B.; Chambers, Jay G.; Guarino,
Cassandra (Eds.)
$54.95 (ISBN 0803966245)

Titles published by Corwin that would be useful in
researching program development include the following:

Professional Development Schools: Weighing the Evidence
Abdal-Haqq, Ismat
Hardcover: $39.95 (ISBN 0803963491)
Paperback: $16.95 (ISBN 0803963505)

*Show Me the Evidence! Proven and Promising Programs
for America's Schools*
Slavin, Robert E.; Fashola, Olatokunbo S.
Hardcover: $49.95 (ISBN 0803967101)
Paperback: $21.95 (ISBN 080396711X)

PubList

http://www.publist.com/

PubList uses sources such as R. R. Bowker's *Books in Print*
and Ulrich's *International Periodicals Directory* to provide bib-
liographic data for more than 150,000 domestic and international print and electronic publications including magazines,
journals, electronic journals, newsletters, and monographs
and hyperlinks to some publishers. This site provides quick
and easy access to detailed publication information. Articles
can be ordered from here as well.

CONCLUSION

Although the Internet offers unlimited resources and information about grantwriting and about locating funding sources, it is sometimes useful to have printed information as well. To locate books about grantwriting or about other aspects of education that would assist in generating ideas about program development, simply turn to the Internet. Online booksellers and educational book publishers provide secured online sales from your home or office, sometimes at a substantial discount, and delivery is usually guaranteed within several days.

If you intend to purchase books with grant funds, these sites can be enormously valuable when developing your budget. At the click of your mouse, you can generate a list of titles and each book's ISBN, author, and price.

9

---•←---

On the Home Front

State Departments of Education

State education department home pages vary greatly. Some are maintained well and are updated frequently; others are not. Educators should visit their state department site regularly to see whether information about grants may be available—many have excellent information about state programs and priorities, hints and tips for grantwriting, names of contacts, current databases of relevant information, and links to other grant sources.

If you don't know how to access your state department of education, finding the address (or URL) can be accomplished in several ways. Using a search engine such as Dogpile (http://www. dogpile.com) is one way, as discussed in Chapter 2. The addresses, or URLs, are often printed on department communications and publications. Another way is to visit the Chief Council of State School Officers' home page.

CHIEF COUNCIL OF STATE SCHOOL OFFICERS

http://www.ccsso.org

The Chief Council of State School Officers (CCSSO) is a nationwide, nonprofit organization composed of the public officials who head departments of elementary and secondary education in the states, the District of Columbia, the Department of Defense Education Activity, and five extrastate jurisdictions. CCSSO's home page provides access to news, priorities, state initiatives, and other items that may be useful to grantwriters. The CCSSO site provides a link (Education Agencies) from its home page that leads to a point-and-click map that links directly to all state education home pages.

THE STATE DEPARTMENT OF EDUCATION WEBSITES

As previously mentioned, the home pages of state departments of education vary greatly, and it can be quite interesting to compare them! Some state education department home pages have direct links to grant information. Ideally, a link (visible and obvious) should exist on the home page, and it should lead to both state and federal grant information, provide application forms that may be downloaded, list contact names and phone numbers, and give other useful information or links for educators who are interested in writing grants, whether a novice or advanced grantwriter. Few states' home pages provide such convenience, however.

At this time, the majority of states have some grant information that is buried within the site and difficult to retrieve. Exploring links with names such as *Programs and Services, For Educators*, or *Initiatives* may lead to some hit-or-miss grant information. In some instances, site searches can yield useful information, but not all state education agency home pages have search capabilities. If an index exists, peruse it. Sometimes, it may be that the only information to be found about grants or funding is contact information (names and telephone numbers) for state initiatives or listings of previously awarded initiatives.

Box 9.1

Keep in mind that student performance data, state demographics, and other information of interest to grantwriters may be accessed from state education office home pages. Also, information on state scholarships, awards, upcoming conferences, or special programs for teachers, administrators, or students may be found.

Sites that are designated with an asterisk provide excellent information that is easy to locate and that may be useful to an experienced, novice, or out-of-state grantwriter. These sites could serve as models for other states that want to provide grant information that effectively reaches its intended audience.

Alabama (http://www.alsde.edu/). Has Awards and Scholarships and Grants links, but little information is provided.

Alaska (http://www.educ.state.ak.us/). Grants and scholarships (links and PDF forms) are listed under Forms and Grants for Districts. Also, Grants for Schools and Districts is a link on the pull-down menu. Good information here.

Arizona (http://www.ade.state.az.us/). Plentiful state grant information can be found under Information and Financial Services.

Arkansas (http://arkedu.state.ar.us/). No direct link to grants, but some state grant information can be found within Director's Memos or by searching site.

California (http://goldmine.cde.ca.gov/). The Grant Information link provides excellent listing of grants available in California. The pull-down menu organizes grants by type, a nice feature.

Colorado (http://www.cde.state.co.us/). Extensive grant information is found by linking on the State and Federal Grants link on the left side of the home page. Grants are organized by state and federal categories.

Connecticut (http://www.state.ct.us/sde/). Limited grant information can be found via the Request for Proposals link. The Grants Management link provides contacts and other information.

Delaware (http://www.doe.state.de.us/). Grant information is very limited, even using DOE search. A few links to grant programs can be found on the "checkerboard" at the bottom of page.

Florida (http://www.firn.edu/doe/index.html). Entitlement and discretionary grant information is found under Information for Educators.

Georgia (http://www.doe.k12.ga.us/). It seems that just about everything appears on this home page except the words grant or funding. A Federal Programs link can be found under the Programs heading. Using the site search will uncover some state information.

Hawaii (http://www.k12.hi.us/). No direct links to grants from the home page, but site search using "grant" yields much information about grants funded in Hawaii.

Idaho (http://www.sde.state.id.us/dept/). Grant link is found under Curriculum and Accountability.

*Illinois (http://www.isbe.state.il.us/). The Grant Opportunities link leads to information on federal, state, and foundation grants. Application forms can be downloaded. Very useful information.

Indiana (http://www.doe.state.in.us). Some grant information can be found buried within the Programs and Services link (left index). Go to the heading Center for Community Relations and Special Populations to find grants for alternative education, for student exploratory teaching, and for education of homeless children and youth. Other grant information is interspersed throughout the site.

Iowa (http://www.state.ia.us/educate/index. html). Easy-to-find links go directly to information on grants and programs and services.

Kansas (http://www.ksbe.state.ks.us/). Awards and Scholarships link on home page is easy to find. A site search yielded great information, especially the KSBE Grant Index.

Kentucky (http://www.kde.state.ky.us/). Go to Grant Opportunities in the pull-down menu at the top of the home page.

Louisiana (http://www.doe.state.la.us/). Has links on the home page to state, regional, and federal grants; find them under Grants & Opportunities.

Maine (http://janus.state.me.us/education/homepage.htm). No convenient link to grants. Some information found via Programs link on left index and the Site Index link.

Maryland (http://www.msde.state.md.us/). Some information found using site search and interspersed under Links for Educators. No direct grants link.

Massachusetts (http://www.doe.mass.edu). State RFPs, awards, grants archives, and administration manuals are found under Grants Information on drop-down menu.

Michigan (http://www.mde.state.mi.us). Grants, state aid, and financial assistance all are found under the Grants and Finances link.

Minnesota (http://www.educ.state.mn.us). Grant information listed under Workshops and Grants (left index).

Mississippi (http://www.mdek12.state.ms.us). Request for Proposals and Resources links lead to information on grants, foundations, and funding resources.

Missouri (http://services.dese.state.mo.us/). Grant information (state and federal) is located under the Programs and Services A-Z and Programs and Initiatives headers. A site search also yields information.

Montana (http://www.metnet.state.mt.us/main.html). Federal Resources link is found on the Education News drop-down menu. Some state grant information can be found by using the OPI Document Search.

Nebraska (http://www.nde.state.ne.us). There is no direct link to grants or funding. A site search yields limited information. A few links exist to specific grant programs.

Nevada (http://www.nsn.k12.nv.us/nvdoe/). No grant information found.

New Hampshire (http://www.ed.state.nh.us/). The Programs and Services Search link (left index) yields indirect grant information. No direct grants links found.

*New Jersey (http://www.state.nj.us/education/). Grants link from home page leads to the department's Office of Grants Management and Development, which offers information on discretionary, entitlement, and federal and state subgrant programs. Key word grant search is easy to use and provides good results.

New Mexico (http://sde.state.nm.us/). No grant information found.

New York (http://www.nysed.gov/). Some grants information found under Program Offices (on the drop-down menu); click on Grants Finance Unit.

North Carolina (http://www.dpi.state.nc.us/). No direct link to grant information exists on the home page. A site search for *grant* yields some current, but very limited, information.

North Dakota (http://www.dpi.state.nd.us/dpi/index.htm). Grant Information link on home page leads to impressive list of technology grants, title program grants, and other grants of interest to in- and out-of-state educators.

Ohio (http://www.ode.state.oh.us/). No direct link to access information about grants. A site search for *grant* does yield current proposal requests and other grant information.

Oklahoma (http://sde.state.ok.us/). A link to state grant applications can be found within the Index—several other links there may prove useful to grantwriters.

Oregon (http://www.ode.state.or.us/). Two links exist on this home page—Resources and Grants link (left column) and Grant Opportunities via scroll down menu.

*Pennsylvania (http://www.pde.psu.edu/). Excellent grants information can be accessed via two fast-find pull-down menus: see the headings Education Reform Initiatives (E-Grants) and The Department of Education (Grants).

Rhode Island (http://www.ridoe.net). Impressive listing of state and federal grants found via the A-Z Site Index (grants).

South Carolina (http://www.state.sc.us/sde/). Grants link is found via Educators link on home page. A site search for *grant* (on home page) also yields useful information.

South Dakota (http://www.state.sd.us/state/executive/ deca/). Link to federal K-12 grants information under Programs and Services.

Tennessee (http://www.state.tn.us/education/). Find state grants by clicking on the Education Initiatives link; useful grantwriting information is found via the For Educators link.

*Texas (http://www.tea.state.tx.us/). The School Finance and Grants and the Grant Information links provide information on state and federal grants. The department's excellent *Grantseeker's Resource Guide* can be found here.

Utah (http://www.usoe.k12.ut.us/). Grants link, under Resources heading, leads to state and federal grant information. Also provides a direct link to the Utah Center for Grant Information and Training at Snow College South.

Vermont (http://www.state.vt.us/educ/). Grant Opportunities link can be found via the Vermont Education Matters link on the home page.

Virginia (http://www.pen.k12.va.us/VDOE/). No direct link. A search of Superintendent's Memos yields current information.

Washington (http://www.k12.wa.us/). No direct grants link, but a site search found various grant-related documents buried within the site.

West Virginia (http://wvde.state.wv.us/). The Ed First/Goals 2000 link provides information on grantwriting workshops that are held annually. A site search for *grant* yielded useful and current information.

Wisconsin (http://www.dpi.state.wi.us/). No direct grants link, but a site search yielded information about several grants.

Wyoming (http://www.k12.wy.us/). Some grant information is found embedded by clicking through the Wyoming Department of Education's Programs and Services link. Site search for *grants* yields some results.

CONCLUSION

State education agencies vary greatly in the amount and type of grant information that they provide. The best sites provide up-to-date information about both state and federal grants, tips on grantwriting, and links to other useful sites.

If you don't know your state education department's address, use a search engine or visit the home page of the Chief Council of State School Officers' site, at http://www.ccsso.org. This site provides up-to-date links to all state education agencies.

Regardless of the type of grant information that is found, most state education sites provide links to student achievement and other data that may be useful to grantwriters. Awards and other program information can be found at most sites also. Take time to visit your own education department's site to review what opportunities are available in your state.

10

Other Internet Applications

Mailing Lists, Discussion Groups, and E-Mail

A good way to solve problems or learn about new topics is by discussing issues and questions with people interested in the same subject. The Internet now provides a means for such individuals to communicate. Newsgroups, e-mailing lists, and discussion groups are not the same as the Internet. Rather, they are services on the Internet, just as the World Wide Web and e-mail are services on the Internet. The Internet contains thousands of special interest groups, and there's something on almost every subject—including grantwriting.

MAILING LISTS

Mailing lists send messages to you through e-mail, and you send messages to the list the same way. Sometimes, discussions are moderated by the list owner, but not always. (Being moderated means that someone sees all the mail first and then decides what will be sent out to the list as a whole.) Someone sends out a message, and it is distributed via e-mail to everybody on the list. Members can reply to the messages, send new messages, or just "lurk," reading the messages without participating. Each time any list member posts a reply, it's distributed via e-mail to everyone else on the list. Some lists can be distributed in digest form, with groups of postings periodically collected into a single large posting with an index. (Rather than five separate messages, one message with the five messages indexed would be received.)

How do these lists work? For a free subscription, you send an e-mail message to the list administrator (this is not actually a person, just an automated system), and your e-mail address is added to the list. A reply is sent that gives all the details about the list and how to participate. (Hint: Save this list information in a separate e-mail folder labeled *Subscription Information* or another appropriate name. Because the procedure for unsubscribing to listservs can vary, it is good to keep this information in a handy place.) If a list does not meet your needs or if the volume of information is too overwhelming, don't hesitate to unsubscribe.

HOW DO YOU FIND OUT ABOUT MAILING LISTS?

Liszt

One way to find out what mailing lists exist is to visit Liszt (http://www.liszt.com), a directory of more than 90,000 Internet discussion groups, mailing lists, newsgroups, and Internet Relay Chat (IRC) channels. A Liszt search using the term *grants* recently revealed a number of matches of interest to grantwriters:

- grantdisc-mg—grantwriting skills workshop forum
- grants—grantwriting
- grants-l—Grants-L mailing list (to promote external funding for international education and research)
- tlcf—technical assistance and discussion for states developing educational technology plans, applying for Technology Literacy Challenge Fund Grants, or both

U.S. Department of Education's EDInfo List

If you are not already receiving EDInfo, put this on your to-do list in order to keep abreast of new information from and initiatives by the U.S. Department of Education. By doing so, you will receive regular updates and progress reports on education initiatives delivered directly to your e-mail address.

Simply start an e-mail message to listproc@inet.ed.gov. Then type *SUBSCRIBE EDINFO YOURFIRSTNAME YOURLASTNAME* in the message. (Turn off any signature blocks.) Then send it! Thus, a person named Sam Adams would simply send this message to listproc@inet.ed.gov:

SUBSCRIBE EDINFO SAM ADAMS

Individuals can search for the following using these links:

- Past EDInfo messages—http://www.ed.gov/MailingLists/EDInfo/
- The archives—http://www.ed.gov/MailingLists/EDInfo/search.html
- Past ED Initiatives—http://www.ed.gov/pubs/EDInitiatives/ (See Figure 10.1 for a sample of a past ED Initiative.)

NEH OUTLOOK

NEH OUTLOOK is a monthly e-mail newsletter of the National Endowment for the Humanities (http://www.neh.gov). To subscribe, send an e-mail to newsletter@neh.gov and type the word *subscribe* in the body of the message. To view past issues, go to http://www. Neh.gov/news/outook/index.html.

Grantseeker Tips

Grantseeker Tips disseminates biweekly tips and ideas for people wanting to successfully pursue grants from founda-

Figure 10.1. An Announcement From a March 24, 2000 ED
Initiatives Message

Smaller Learning Communities

Regional workshops are being offered on the Smaller
Learning Communities Program. This new program offers
$45 million in competitive grants to help school districts
plan, develop, implement, or expand smaller, more personal "learning communities" (600 students maximum) in
large high schools (1,000 students or more). Strategies supported under the program may include, but are not limited
to, the creation of . . .

> small learning clusters, career academies, magnet schools,
> or other approaches to creating schools-within-schools;
> block scheduling; personal adult advocates, teacher-advisory
> systems, and other mentoring strategies; and reduced
> teaching loads.

The workshops will provide superintendents and other
district educators a chance to learn from researchers,
experts, and practitioners experienced in developing
smaller learning communities. Places and dates include . . .

> New York City on March 23; Los Angeles on March 29;
> Houston on March 30; Albuquerque on March 31; Chi-
> cago on April 4; and Wausau (WI) on April 26.

To ensure availability of space, please pre-register
(online) for the sessions at http://www.dtiassociates.com/
smallschools

For details, please see:
http://www.ed.gov/offices/OESE/SLCP/outreach1.html
http://www.ed.gov/offices/OESE/SLCP/

tions, corporations, and government agencies. Drawing from first-hand grant experience, owners/editors Lynn and Jeremy Miner share clever tips that cover all aspects of planning and writing proposals: identifying funding sources, making preproposal contacts, technical writing tips, and document design. To subscribe, simply send an e-mail to *LynnMiner@ Marquette.edu* and enter *join* in the subject line.

SchoolGrants

http://www.schoolgrants.org/

Advertising itself as "your one-stop site for K-12 grant opportunities," this site has numerous resources, including a free monthly electronic newsletter. Much information is available for locating, writing, receiving, and managing grant proposals. Links are given to grant-related state and federal agencies as well as private foundations.

Usenet News Groups or Discussion Groups

This is a NETwork of individual USErs, hence *Usenet*, an electronic bulletin board and discussion area accessed by an estimated 24 million people. People can post messages to the group and read or reply to the messages. (Obviously, the value of the information is only equal to the reliability of an author.) Such groups are typically less scholarly than listserv groups.

You can ask (or post) questions, read articles, and write your own messages. At deja.com's USENET discussion group (http://www.deja.com/usenet/), there are more than 80,000 discussion forums. A search for the term *grants* yielded more than 3,000 hits. Unfortunately for grantseekers, many of these hits uncover individuals needing grants or an alternate form of the word *grant* (e.g., *migrants*). Some foundation and government information is available here, however.

Other discussion groups include the following:

- RemarQ at http://www.remarq.com
- Talk City at http://www.talkcity.com
- VP Mail at http://www.list.to

ScienceWise.com

http://www.sciencewise.com

ScienceWise.com and Webfonia have partnered to offer powerful grant search tools via links to MOLIS, (ScienceWise) Alert, and FEDIX, which are found at the bottom of the home page. Also found on the home page is an easy-to-use Search for Funding tool that utilizes keyword and funding-type descriptors.

ScienceWise Alert is a free e-mail service that automatically delivers research and education funding opportunities within your targeted areas of interest. Once registered, you will receive periodic e-mail messages according to the areas selected.

FEDIX provides direct links to grant and research information from participating federal agencies—the Office of Naval Research, the Department of Defense, the National Institutes of Health, the U.S. Department of Agriculture, the Agency for International Development, the Air Force Office of Scientific Research, and NASA.

MOLIS, or the Minority On-Line Information Service, provides services that promote education, research, and diversity on a national level for minority institutions in partnership with government, industry, and other sectors. Scholarship and fellowship information for minorities can also be found here.

COLLABORATING FROM A DISTANCE? NO PROBLEM!

E-Mail

Grantwriters must sometimes overcome problems of geography and time, but with e-mail and the ability to share files, teams can write proposals from diverse locations. E-mail can assist grantwriters in a number of phases throughout a grantwriting cycle. For example, it can help to gauge the preliminary interest of individuals or agencies in working on a collaborative project, to assist in brainstorming before or during the grantwriting process; to request letters of support; to collaborate on actual grantwriting by sending files or sections of information; or to collect formative and summative data from program participants as a part of the evaluation process. Program managers will want to know how to develop distribution lists to keep committees and participants informed at the touch of a button!

File Storage

Another related service new to the Internet is free file storage. Sites such as I-drive (http://www.idrive.com) allow you to save information on their company servers (after registering, of course). Your stored files are accessible to you from any Internet location, and you may allow others to either view or access them.

Videoconferences

If videoconferencing is in your future, whether as a grantwriter, project director, or participant, check out the videoconferencing atlas developed by SAVIE, the Support Action to Facilitate the Use of Videoconferencing in Education, at http://www.savie.com.

Online Philanthropy Matches

Grantmakers have a presence on the Web . . . and grantseekers look for funders on the Web. It was only a matter of time until a company ingeniously matched the needs of the two, allowing verified nonprofits and public schools to submit proposals online directly into the database of member foundation grantmakers. Billing itself as the "first online philanthropy web portal," CyberGrants (http://www.cybergrants.com) acts as an intermediary, allowing educators and grantseekers from other nonprofits to research grant guidelines and create, maintain, and submit online proposals.

Grantmaking organizations may find using the services of CyberGrants very appealing. In addition to providing an immediate presence on the Internet, the service promises less paperwork and increased speed and efficiency, thereby allowing more time to build philanthropic relationships. CyberGrants also offers a comprehensive grants management database, including budgeting, payment scheduling, tracking, reporting, and automated notifications capabilities. Web-based pricing is calculated on the basis of number of users, technical support level, and total annual-giving budget.

CONCLUSION

What could be more convenient than finding out about new grant and funding opportunities by having them delivered to your e-mail address regularly—for free! Take advantage of these services offered by government agencies and private sources.

Although most of us think of the Internet as being only the World Wide Web, it offers many other functions and applications. From e-mail to videoconferences to discussion groups, the Internet can assist the grantwriter and grant manager in numerous ways.

11

When the Pencil
Meets the Paper

Online Grantwriting Tips

A funder's printed guidelines will tell you what you need to include in your grant proposal. Once you've identified a funding source and are ready to write a proposal, you can turn to the Internet for assistance and tips on the grantwriting process.

Although some sites are more subject specific than others (e.g., technology, research), the ideas and methods can usually apply to other topics because most funders request substantially the same information, even if they use different words or ask questions in a different order. A common rule for all grantwriters is to follow all instructions explicitly.

To learn from the experiences (or mistakes) of others, check the sites in this chapter for grantwriting hints and tips:

10-POINT PLAN FOR STANDARD GRANT-FUNDING PROPOSAL

http://www.npguides.org/grant.htm

This site includes sample cover letters, private grant applications, budgets, and other items of interest to grantwriters.

WRITING A SUCCESSFUL GRANT PROPOSAL

http://www.mcf.org/mcf/grant/writing.htm

Minnesota Council on Foundations provides excellent information for and about nonprofits in the state. FAQs include pros and cons of hiring a professional grantwriter and what to do if a proposal is funded.

A GUIDE TO PROPOSAL PLANNING AND WRITING

http://www.oryxpress.com/miner.htm

This guide by Jeremy T. Miner and Lynn E. Miner offers extensive tips for grantwriters. Included are hints for document formatting, such as the use of bold headings and white space. Their suggestions include contacting not only former grantees (a list of questions to ask is supplied) but also grant reviewers.

LUCENT TECHNOLOGIES WAVELAN USA EDUCATION PROGRAM

http://www.wavelan.com/education/pdfs/grantwriting.pdf

Lucent Technologies offers an excellent 30-page grantwriting guide. It was designed for technology projects, but the information can be easily adapted to any project. (Information abounds on how educational institutions can acquire the necessary tools to implement wireless data networking that facilitates the educational process.)

PROPOSAL WRITING: INTERNET RESOURCES

http://www.library.wisc.edu/libraries/Memorial/ grants/proposal.htm

This site from the University of Wisconsin—Madison lists approximately 20 links to excellent grantwriting resources, some of which are especially designed for research proposals.

GRANT RESOURCES

http://www.proposalwriter.com/grants.html

Deborah Kluge, an independent writing consultant from Columbia, Maryland, has compiled an extensive online list of links of interest to grantwriters. Also included are specialized government contracting and grant resources for small, minority, women-owned, and other disadvantaged businesses. This is a very comprehensive site. Her proposal writing tips and a free proposal checklist are found as links on the left index of the home page.

D.O.E. CARLSBAD AREA OFFICE AND WESTINGHOUSE WASTE ISOLATION DIVISION: TECHNOLOGY TRANSFER AND ECONOMIC DEVELOPMENT PROGRAM (TTED)

http://www.t2ed.com

The Carlsbad Area Office of the U.S. Department of Energy and the Waste Isolation Division of the Westinghouse Electric

Company of Morrison Knudsen Corporation have funded technologies that are available for transfer to the private sector for commercialization, research, or internal use at no cost. (The only requirement is that you receive authorization to use the document.) Of the approximately 20 programs available for transfer, three are of direct interest to grantwriters or those who provide programs about grantwriting. They are as follows:

1. *Grant Proposal Self-Assessment Tool* (GrantSAT)
2. *Writing Winning Grant Proposals I* (WWGP I)
3. *Writing Winning Grant Proposals II* (WWGP II)

GrantSAT helps grantwriters evaluate and improve their grant proposals using 75 criteria grouped in nine categories, which are as follows:

1. General style and content

2. Cover letter and executive summary

3. Problem statement and needs assessment

4. Objectives and benefits

5. Qualifications

6. Methods

7. Budget

8. Evaluation

9. Conclusion and attachments

GrantSAT provides feedback by criterion, by category, and by the document as a whole.

INNOVATION NETWORK, INC.

http://www.innonet.org/

Innonet, which bills itself as "the most unique workstation available on the Internet," allows users to create six products: strategic program maps, optional action steps, budgets, evaluation plans, fundraising action plans, and grant applications. Log on as a new user to access WIN!, a workstation for innovative nonprofits that provides users with free online tools to assist program managers. The Strategic Program Map, completed online, helps to identify mission, goals, objectives, activities, and outcomes—key elements in organizing and managing grant projects or nonprofit associations. Excellent information on qualitative data collection can be found at the Repair Center and via Tools and Links. Explanations are provided on appropriate data collection methods, such as surveys, interviews, and focus groups; how to collect information; and how to interpret and report it. Sample surveys and online grant application forms are also found here.

GUIDE FOR WRITING A FUNDING PROPOSAL

http://www.canr.msu.edu/aee/dissthes/proposal.htm

S. Joseph Levine has created an easy-to-follow proposal guide that provides both instructions on how to write a funding proposal and actual examples of a completed proposal.

Box 11.1

Many of the federal program sites offer hints and tips on proposal writing. The following is excerpted from the Fund for the Improvement of Postsecondary Education site at http://www.ed.gov/offices/OPE/FIPSE/steps. html.

"Funding Your Best Ideas: A 12-Step Program"
by Joan Straumanis

Part I—Before Writing

1. Innovate—and if you can't think of anything brand new, do something unexpected. This is your angle; now feature it.

2. Do your homework. Find your niche. What are others doing about this issue? Show that you know, and place your project within this context.

3. Build a team. Mix things up. Build and cross bridges—among departments, disciplines, and schools. Between academia and business. Between schools and colleges. Include students and administrators. Be generous: share work and ownership. Appoint an advisory committee of famous people in your field—to get a head start on dissemination—but don't give them much work to do, and you won't need to pay them very much.

4. Find the right funding agency. Know agency interests, culture, and style. Submit applications to more than one agency (but, of course, don't accept multiple grants supporting the same activities).

5. Use the phone. Call a program officer, briefly summarize your idea, and prepare specific questions.

Box 11.1 *continued*

Take the program officers's advice very seriously, but exercise your own best judgment. Some agencies are more directive than others.

Part II—While Writing

6. Use a journalistic writing style. Use the "W" words of journalism: Who, what, when, where, why, and how. Also use bullets, lists, outlines, diagrams, and tables. Don't obsess on any topic, even if important. Make it interesting; let every sentence do a job. Assume that your reviewer is reading in bed, falling asleep—which is very likely true.

7. Follow guidelines to the letter. Keep them before you as you write (but don't quote them back to the agency). Match headings in the proposal to headings in the guidelines so the reader doesn't have to hunt for needed information. Use "signposts:" I am about to explain why . . . I have just argued that . . .

8. Build in continuation, evaluation, and dissemination. Factory installed, not an add-on and not postponed to the last year. Continuation plans are an indicator of institutional commitment. Evaluation should be independent and objective, but doesn't need to meet standards of the Journal of Psychometrics—use common sense. What would you want to know about the success of an idea before you would consider adopting it? Evaluate "politically"(i.e., with an eye toward later publicity). What would you want to see in headlines? Note the difference between passive and active dissemination. (The first disseminates admiration, not innovation.)

Box 11.1 *continued*

9. Watch the bottom line. Share costs. Know how to cut costs without hurting the project: request replacement salaries instead of released time, charge actual instead of estimated benefits, follow agency recommendations on indirect costs.

10. Leverage funds. Solicit funds from third parties, contingent on grant funding. This can be done in advance (to beef up cost share and make proposal more attractive), as well as after project is funded.

11. Get a sharp (toothed) reader. Best: someone unfamiliar with your field, your project. Not an editor/proofreader. Have them read final draft without taking notes. Then ask them to tell you—from memory—what the project will do, how it will do it, why it is significant, and how it is different. Rewrite proposal if these answers aren't clear and correct, or if they don't flow effortlessly.

12. Write the abstract last. Put in your key innovation. Write 3 versions: one page (first page of proposal, whether requested or not), one paragraph (if requested), and one line, the proposal title—which you should think of as a mini-abstract (descriptive and intriguing). Don't repeat abstract or proposal text. Prepare for the possibility that some sleepy reviewer might read only the abstract.

—Joan Straumani
FIPSE Program Officer

Index